INTEGRATED FORCE PROJECTION BY INDIA

INTEGRATED FORCE PROJECTION BY INDIA

Brig Sukhdeep Sangwan

Published in association with
Centre For Joint Warfare Studies (CENJOWS)
Kashmir House, Rajaji Marg, New Delhi

Vij Books India Pvt Ltd
Ansari Road, Daryaganj, New Delhi

Published   by

Vij Books India Pvt Ltd
(Publishers, Distributors & Importers)
2/19, Ansari Road, Darya Ganj
New Delhi - 110002
Phones: 91-11-43596460, 91-11- 65449971
Fax: 91-11-47340674
www.vijbooks.com
e-mail : vijbooks@rediffmail.com

ISBN: 978-93-80177-42-7

Contents

Foreword

It is a matter of great pleasure for me to be writing the foreword for this book which essentially focuses on a subject that entails true integration of all elements of national power and does not confine merely to the vividly accepted belief of use of armed forces alone for force projection assignments. The definition of force projection is still subject to some debate since generally accepted norms and yardsticks focusing on the use of military muscle for projecting force do merit review. Contrast this belief with the constituency of propounder of a synergized application of numerous components and constituents that have the potential to catalyse the entire process of force projection.

The study attempts to highlight the fact that a mere congregation of soldiers, sailors and airmen do not make a regional power. It rightly emphasizes, without wandering on the fringes of any blustering rhetoric or puffery, that proverbial synergy is an elemental imperative for force projection. The book stresses that the traditional view of security and force projection focused on mere application of hard power has to give way to the new concept that entails a true amalgam of political, economic, diplomatic, environmental, social and military dimensions. It is only then that India would rise to global prominence and incontestable regional dominance.

The nation needs to recognize that rigorous thinking and discussions are needed to evolve a truly integrated organizational set up that would steer us on the right course to our pre-ordained rise to such prominence. Towards that end, the study rightfully recommends greater integration of defence forces with various ministeries for effective, frictionless and well modulated options for force projection that would afford a platform for various think tanks and strategists to analyse them and facilitate the process of evolution of a force projection doctrine for the country.

I would like to congratulate the author, Brigadier Sukhdeep Sangwan, for a well researched study that combines scholastic aphorism with logical subtleties. He succeeds in drawing the attention of readers to the perceptions and nuances that govern the force projection matrix and recommends certain models and structures that would propel our prognostic ascendency to regional supremacy through integrated force projection capabilities. I also wish to compliment Ms Shivani Bhardwaj for her laudatory efforts and effectual research capabilities that have helped immensely in completion of this research.

I am sure "Integrated Force Projection by India" will make an interesting reading and elicit critical evaluation and analysis from all quarters to pave the way for enunciation of a Force Projection Doctrine at the national level.

New Delhi
December 2010

(K B Kapoor)
Maj Gen (Retd)

Preface

All wars are follies, very expensive and very mischievous ones. In my opinion, there never was a good war or a bad peace. When will mankind be convinced and agree to settle their difficulties by arbitration?

- Benjamin Franklin

For a state that achieved its independence by peaceful means and often stood by its commitment and belief to peaceful resolution of disputes, it may sound naive to think of treading into the domain of "Power Projection" to attain the status of a regional power. However, when analysed in the backdrop of historical conundrum that in the past four centuries India's influence in Asia had reached two distinct peaks; one under the Mughals, when India was one of Asia's two dominant cultural and economic powers; and the other, when under the British rule it became the Center of Pan Asian Empire - both of which are suggestive of a safe conclusion that India certainly has the potential to assert itself as a regional power. This realization about its enormous potential and capabilities dawned upon the Indian psyche somewhere in early Eighties when Soviets invaded Afghanistan and the US, China and Pakistan not only covertly colluded against the Soviets but also tried to deny India its natural position as a dominant power in South Asia. Simultaneously, the resurrection of militancy in Punjab, blatant occupation of Indian territorial regions by Pakistan in Siachen and rising atrocities against Tamils in Sri Lanka forced India to pursue a policy of regional dominance. This policy became evident with the launch of Integrated Guided Missile

Development Program (IGMDP), substantial increase in Indian defence spending wherein the defence budget more than doubled from $4.09 billion in 1980 to $ 9.89 billion in 1988-89 and by the use of military power in Sri Lanka and Maldives. This activism clearly signalled the arrival of India into the domain of power projection and assertion as a regional power. Thus, after more than half a century of false starts, disappointing take-offs and unrealized potential, India is now emerging as the swing state in the global balance of power. In the current century, it will have enough opportunities to influence some of the critical and pressing issues related to the regional stability, geo-political alliances and apt management of globalization issues.

India, undisputedly will emerge as an unparalleled and peerless regional and economic power by the year 2020. Its regional cooperation and understanding with Russia and China may, in all likelihood, form a de-facto "geo-strategic" alliance that would openly challenge the US's 'larger than life' image as the dominant power. India will remain in the fore-front of this alliance by virtue of its geo-strategic location and socio-economic reforms. It will draw its strength from stable and strong democratic set up, sound and ascendant economic stability and above all, an apolitical military set up which serves as a powerful tool at the hands of the polity for projecting the nation's claim as a regional power.

With such a vibrant and quivering democracy suitably aided by resonant and enthralling patriotism, India has all the ingredients of being assigned the coveted status of a regional power. Our quick response to the Asian Tsunami in Andaman & Nicobar Islands, evacuation of trapped Indians from Middle East and deft handling of pirates in the Gulf region have all but contributed in cementing our claims of sound force projection capabilities, both in intent and content. We now have to develop our capabilities in consonance with our aspirations to achieve due status in the region. While at the national level this would entail a synergized application of the nation's wherewithal, in the military context it translates into the ability of Indian

Defence Forces to undertake operations away from the mainland so as to convincingly project India's Comprehensive National Power (CNP) and consolidate its case for being recognized as a regional power. Such operations would entail a tri-service or bi-service joint force operating for a reasonably long period of time without the close support inherent in operations on the mainland. Such operations encompass a wide range of activities wherein the military instrument of national power is used in ways other than large scale conventional combat operations usually associated with war. Notwithstanding the small size of force levels and scale of operations these are meant to serve the strategic goals of the nation. The government of the day will have to give specific and explicit orders for such operations after evaluating the strategic objectives and the desired end state. Hence, these operations are strategic in nature irrespective of the size of the force. However, application of the combat power will be planned in detail at the operational and tactical levels.

For all such operations, speedy processing of information, prompt and sound decision making and flawless execution of plans are vital and crucial parameters. The armed forces will therefore have to shoulder heavy and cumbrous responsibility of meticulously planning such joint operations to avoid harum-scarum, erratic and impulsive response to such international calls wherein nation's image as an emerging regional power is at stake. Its time therefore, to study and evaluate various attempts at force projection by developed nations. India surely and certainly needs to safeguard its strategic interests by addressing the long term challenges based on lessons from various models adopted by other states. It has to acknowledge that synergy and jointmanship through seamlessly planned and executed operations from land, sea and air are the sole options for furthering India's cause of projecting itself as a regional power. It has, of course, to be suitably complemented by a stable government and a gregarious and dynamic bureaucratic set up, besides a vibrant economy that would act as a catalyst to boost her claim as a regional power. We can don the mantle of such a power only once we shed our inward looking, reactive, sub continental mindset and start deliberating on pro active options in an exponential manner and not merely in an incremental form since considerable changes are taking place at the global and regional fora.

The aim of this study is to recommend measures that would facilitate the senior leadership in evolving appropriate strategy and a suitable doctrine for force projection in the Indian context.

Before venturing into the domain of making recommendations for the policy makers it would be appropriate to sneak a look into India's historical past which is replete with examples where India has had its share of opportunities in projecting itself at the regional and international levels during the reins of Ashoka the Great, Chandragupta Maurya and the likes; as also during the British rule when it had its share of representation during the two World Wars as part of the Colonial Forces. Post independence also, India has never shirked from its responsibilities at the international arena. Not only did it send its contingent far off to Congo in 1964, but was also seminal in creation of the new nation of Bangladesh closer home. It responded promptly in intervening in Maldives and Sri Lankan crises at the behest of their governments in the1980s. It has been an active participant in the UN Peace Keeping operations and has been a regular subscriber to various missions. It has thus been a gradual process spread over a very long period during which India has projected its intentions of staking its rightful claim as a regional power. Now the time has come when the consolidation phase has to commence and the nation has to formulate suitable force projection policies, strategy and doctrine to announce its arrival as a dominant regional power that is knocking at the doors of being christened as a force to reckon with at the international domain.

Changing global security environment and its impact on South Asia and IOR regions needs to be studied and analysed in detail. The impact of these changes on the future contours of India's security concerns cannot be ignored. A vast array of emerging global, regional, sub-regional and internal complexities enjoin upon India to develop matching military capabilities in consonance with its growing socio-political, economic and technological prowess. While it is fully acknowledged that our national security policy is based on two cardinal principles of *"no extra territorial ambitions"* and *"no ambitions to transplant our ideology on others"*, we must not remain nonchalant and indifferent to our expected role and contributions in global affairs in these difficult moments when uncivil, impudent, insolently disrespectful and shamelessly presumptuous divisive forces are denting and challenging the very foundations of a peaceful civilization world over. We have always risen to such challenges and have been a major and substantial contributor to UN missions. Not only have we acquired an enviable reputation for professionalism mixed with compassion but are also being approached by a number of countries for training their rank and file in undertaking such operations. We now have to graduate from mere contributors to peace keeping missions to the status of a regional power that is capable of projecting itself at the 'global playgrounds'.

Therefore, in keeping with our global and regional aspirations we need to possess capabilities to deploy our joint task forces with clinical precision and nonpareil professionalism. The three services have already embarked on achieving synergy and jointness in various operational, training and administrative facets so as to develop such capabilities. The structures are already in place for joint intelligence, planning and conduct of operations at the highest levels. Requisite interaction at various hierarchical levels amongst the three services conjures up harmony and jointmanship and certainly consolidates our belief in our potential capabilities. Moreover, formulation and up-gradation of our operational doctrines such as Joint Doctrine, Doctrine for Amphibious Operations, Asymmetrical Warfare Doctrine, Special Forces Operations Doctrine etc are all but indicators of our resolve to ensure that our war fighting machinery is not only compatible with futuristic battle scenario but is also capable of undertaking force projection operations in terms of Out of Area Contingencies, Effect

Based Operations, Peace Keeping Missions, Disaster Relief Operations et el. We have to be prepared to address these multi spectrum challenges without diluting our conventional commitments and territorial defence needs. To address these challenges and multi spectrum requirements we definitely need to put in place an Integrated Force Projection Doctrine that should govern the *modus vivendi* for employing the services to translate India's regional and global aspirations into the realms of acceptance at the international forum.

We need to rummage around and find out, whether or not, there is a need to have an integrated force projection doctrine for furthering India's aspirations to become a global or a regional power. Therefore, an endeavour will be made to recommend a coherent and comprehensive Integrated Force Projection option in Indian Context so that it facilitates the formulation of the Doctrine on the said subject.

-Author

CHAPTER 1

SECURITY CHALLENGES IN THE NEW MILLENNIUM

"The true might of a nation is to be sought for not so much in the strength of its army which is but the means of materialising this might, but in the health of its spirit, that it has the will (National Will) to protect it from dangers - external and internal."

- Major General JFC Fuller

India is a paradox, a seemingly impoverished country that was raked by unemployment, poverty and population explosions during its post independence infancy; a country plagued by separatism, internal disturbances, insurgency, terrorism and political instability during its formative years till eighties and nineties; and most recently, a country sending out signals of a stable, orderly, peaceful and progressive India studded with sound political resurgence, strong economic reforms suggestive of a dynamic nation leaping forward to make its mark in the international arena. India's physical vastness, vibrant democracy, sound economic reforms, immense socio cultural resilience and the inability of numerous foreign aided separatist movements to derail its all round progress have strengthened India's aim to be christened as a regional power. Today, India is certainly in the throes of a challenge to the world community to question its growing role in the changing world order. An Indian anthropologist Mr MN

Srinivas has aptly observed, "Indians are actually living in a revolution, although it is not always recognised by many of them nor, for that matter, by the outside world"[1]. It clearly indicates that in a world of imploding and dividing states, rising fundamentalist trends and growing fissiparous tendencies it is important that India is given credit for its generally peaceful resolutions, unblemished human rights record and an enviable non aligned stature that has given it immense strength to stand on its own and stake claim for recognition as an emerging power on the canvas of world affairs. This certainly needs to be factored into the moral intangibles that contribute to a balanced estimate of India's strength and weaknesses especially in view of the security challenges that it faces in the new millennium.

Threats like a series of low intensity conflicts characterised by tribal, ethnic, and left wing movements, as also, the proxy war conducted by Pakistan and various radical jehadi outfits through instrumentality of terrorism are the realities that stare at India without even a blink. India is also affected by the trafficking in drugs and proliferation of small arms and the fact that it is surrounded by two neighbours with nuclear weapons and missiles and history of past aggressions and war. There is also the ever present possibility of hostile radical fundamentalist elements gaining access to the weapons of mass destruction in Pakistan. The country has already experienced four major conventional border wars besides an undetected war in Kargil. India's response to these threats and challenges has always been restrained, measured and moderate in keeping with its peaceful outlook and reputation as a peace loving country.

Thus far, India's strategic policy has been reactive and responsive, be it against external aggression and threats or against the subversive internal disturbances. Our inward looking policies,

---

[1] MN Srinivas, "On Living in a Revolution", in James P Roach, ed, India 2000: The Next Fifteen Years (riverdale, Md Riverdale, 1986), p4

including reluctance to strengthen military potential, had essentially set India on a defensive and reactive path till it suffered a humiliating setback during the Chinese aggression of 1962. The stage for transition had been set since then and the defence became a high priority from 1962 to 1974, when India leaped into the elite club of "nuclear haves" after the 1974 Pokhran Test. Its capabilities have increased over the years as it has moved ponderously and effectively towards an assertive power capable of imposing itself whenever situation so demands. This has been amply demonstrated in the 1971 Indo-Pak war which showcased its military might; IPKF intervention in Sri Lanka in 1980s which showed India's potential in terms of a 'three front' capability; prompt response to the Maldivian crisis that cemented India's stature as a regional power, massive evacuation of civilians from the Gulf in 1990 which showed its capability for a rapid response and most recently, deft handling of Tsunami that highlighted its disaster relief capabilities. Moreover, the successful culmination of Kargil operations has demonstrated that India has begun to launch well coordinated and synergised politico-military and diplomatic offensive to thwart any external aggression.

Today, India rightfully stands at the doorsteps of a new geo-strategic gateway that will enable it to face the security challenges in the new millennium. It has to realize that the future battlefield scenario would be significantly different from that of the past wherein success will largely be dependent on joint teamwork. Battles and wars will be won only once the ground, maritime and air forces operate jointly in pursuit of a commonly shared military objective. There is a need to have a mutual confidence and a shared understanding of the roles played by each service. A close integration during training, exercises, operations, and in the manner in which defence is organised, supported and managed at various levels will go a long way in consolidating jointness, more so, because India is increasingly being seen and respected as an emerging regional power in the multi-polar world of today. If we are to enhance our status in the comity of

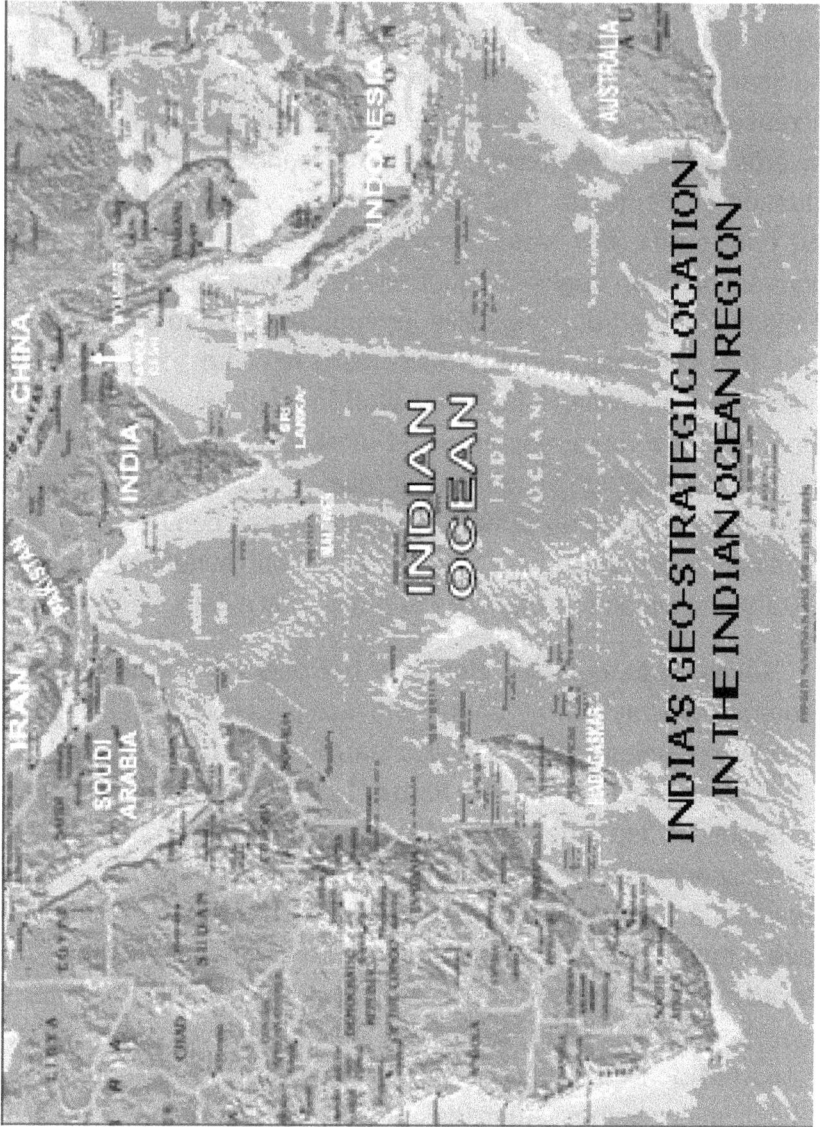

INDIA'S GEO-STRATEGIC LOCATION IN THE INDIAN OCEAN REGION

nations, it will certainly require an integrated and unified approach at all levels. We must think and act together, as a nation, so as to face the emerging security challenges. Integration, therefore, should not be confined merely to military tactics, but should be seen in the widest possible context encompassing the entire wherewithal at the disposal of the nation state. We have to ensure that the concept of jointness and integration does not remain confined to the realms of fantasy and hope, but is translated into reality.[2] We have to assertively announce and let it be known to both; the continental Asia as well as the Indian Ocean Region (IOR) that India cannot be ignored anymore. Its peninsular shape, as seen in the map, assigns it a coastline of approximately 7600 kms and an Exclusive Economic Zone (EEZ) of over two million sq kms. It dominates, or at least influences, most vital sea lanes in the IOR region stretching from Suez Canal and Persian Gulf to the Straits of Malacca through which much of the oil from the Gulf transits. This is an area that has attracted super power rivalries in the past and continues to be a region of heightened activity by extra regional navies on account of current global security concerns. In view of this strategic spread, it is essential for the country to maintain a credible land, air and maritime force to safeguard its security interests. Therefore, the time has come when India has to come out with its declaratory strategic doctrine and a strategic vision for the Twenty First century, or at least for the first quarter till 2020-25 to clearly address the security concerns and the dominant role that it can play in the region. The political leadership has to evolve a penetrative foresight to lead India to its aspirations of becoming a regional power, if not a global one, in the backdrop of its geo-strategic location. The political leadership must accord utmost priority to national security. A resolute, forceful, assertive and determined set-up needs to be put in place to guide and steer an integrated national effort

---

[2] Excerpts from the Address by Defence Minister at the first Advisory Board Meeting of the Centre for Joint Warfare Studies (CENJOWS), New Delhi, 2007.

towards achieving bold, audacious and well defined objectives in keeping with the geo-strategic location and the regional status that the nation enjoys today.

Though the cold war may be over, but the last decade or so has been characterised by numerous strategic developments. The spread of fundamentalism and the terrorist attacks like 9/11 and 26/11 have brought about a greater international convergence on global security issues and challenges. While significant differences of opinions and perceptions remain, there has been a change in diplomatic power equations around the world. Certain quarters may be propagating that the world has become unipolar but in actual fact, this appears to be a transient stage. In the coming decade or so, the world order will, in all probability, stabilize into a multi-polar environment wherein countries like US, EU, Japan and BRIC countries are likely to play dominant roles. Developments like the war on Iraq may certainly have altered many equations in the Middle East; the proliferation and stand off over Iran and North Korea may definitely have influenced several diplomatic alignments; the USA's Af-Pak policy may have certainly raised many eyebrows; and the so called "demise" of LTTE may have certainly dented the morale of similar movements around the world, but one thing which has emerged almost undisputedly, is the rise of Asia as a major power centre in the new world order.

The gradual but distinctly discernible shift towards multi-polarity in power equations and the shift in global Centre of Gravity to Asia are the most distinct realities of this change. This power shift can be attributed to the phenomenal economic rise of the continent over the past few decades. The rise of China and India on the global economic canvas is the most visible manifestation of the forces of globalisation. These developments will certainly have a considerable effect on the socio economic developments and the security scenario in the region. Besides that, this region is also the fountainhead of fundamentalism and global terrorism. All these factors will have a direct bearing on India whose inherent strength and sound democratic credentials make it an important pillar of stability in the Asian region as well as in the emerging world order.

Certainly, the South Asian region today portends to be the vortex of the emergent realpolitik in the new world order of multi polarity and multiple alliances. It's a glaring fact that this region is vulnerable to be exploited by the dominant powers due to the overwhelming asymmetry in the power relations between the South Asian nations where each neighbour looks at the other as a 'suspicious' power. This precipitate fear stems due to the lack of a 'strategic vision' amongst the South Asian nations who prefer to remain insular with nationalistic mindset that chaffs any thought of a regional forum suitably steered by a dominant power. Their fears that India stands in this region as a beacon of democracy amongst a multitude of human diversity and economic disparity pose immense hindrance in continuing any worthwhile alliance in the region that could pose any challenge to the dominant super power in the world. Our national objective therefore should be two fold; first – to gain confidence of our neighbours by assuring them of our genuineness as a dominant benevolent power by virtue of its geo strategic location and cultural affinity with each of these neighbours, and second – to promote India as an eminent regional power by 2020 by integrating and influencing our extended neighbourhood through political, economic and military diplomacy. We need to dispel any apprehensions of hegemonic tendencies in the minds of our neighbours through confidence building measures. Equipped perhaps with the most powerful and free media that can be intelligently utilized to project our national interests, India needs to cap all its inadequacies and project strategies that cement its claims as a regional power. It certainly needs to evolve a doctrine that comprehensively facilitates it to project itself as a force to reckon with; a force that is here to stay through the twenty first century; a force that will dictate the geo strategic dimensions in the entire region by projecting itself, with propensity, as a competing force capable of challenging major powers. It has to project itself as the predominant power in the Indian sub-continent. It already is a power in terms of size, natural resources and human capital. It has an unabridged and unassailable lead in the sub-continent in terms of economy, industrial development, infrastructure and hi-technology wherewithal. Unfortunately, it has not been able to project itself as the predominant military power, especially so, because Pakistan has been built up as the 'regional spoiler' state by the West and by China in terms of nuclear weapons and missile arsenal.[3] India needs to project itself as one of the three major powers in Asia, besides China and Japan. It has to build its Force Projection capabilities at an accelerated pace by exploiting its strategic strength and geo political dominance in the region. Military preponderance in both the nuclear and conventional military fields needs to be built to add teeth to its force projection capabilities. In terms of quantification, it should have an overwhelming military superiority in South Asia and relative parity with China.

All these are essential when we analyse the contours of our regional trends and security concerns in the immediate future. A brief analysis of the following regional trends will help us in understanding the security scenario that stares at us and will influence our destiny over the course of next few years:

West Asia

West Asia remains one of the most unstable, conflict prone and volatile regions of the world. This region has the potential to remain a future source of conflict; at least till the Palestine problem is resolved. Coupled with this, the stability and security in the Gulf region is crucial to India as it has an impact on India's economy as well as on the safety of a large Indian Diaspora.

Central Asian Region

The Central Asian region has witnessed increased engagement

---

[3] Dr Subhash Kapila, "India's Defence Policies and Strategic Thought: A Comparative Analysis", 2003.

by the US, China and Russia. Moreover, the countries of this region, all of which broke away from the erstwhile Soviet Union, are fledgling economies and have nascent governing structures which make them a potential source of conflict. India, therefore, cannot remain oblivious of this region in its North and the politico-strategic developments thereof.

South Asian Region

The enhanced economic strength of ASEAN countries and the importance of this region, especially the Straits of Malacca for transit of global trade and energy, have resulted in India actively pursuing its "Look East" policy since it shares common concerns on a range of security challenges like terrorism, religious radicalism of ideologies, gun running, drugs, piracy and illegal migration.[4] While India could not become a member of ASEAN which was established in 1967, it joined the new entity, the ASEAN Regional Forum (ARF) which came into existence in 1993. The aim of joining this forum was to be a part of the security related discussions and deliberations of the region but the group has so far refrained from discussing any contentious issues. Another organization, the Shanghai Cooperation Organization (SCO) came up in 2006, pointedly for looking into issues of regional terrorism and Islamic extremism. India has an observer status with SCO. East Asia Summit, set up in 2005, is yet another entity with sixteen members including India. It's not yet clear what East Asia Summit is set to achieve but one thing is clear: the emergence of these organizations signifies that the Asian countries increasingly feel the need for a collective identity to forge cooperative common policies which will keep in mind the interests of each nation. In due course of time, it may lead to the constitution of an Asian Union on the lines of European Union;

---

[4] http://www.idsa.in/publications/JDS/2.2/article1.pdf, Changing Global Security Environment with Specific Reference to Our Region and its Impact on the Indian Army.

but right now, given the mutual rivalries, fears and aspirations, the prospects are nowhere in sight. By being accorded a place in all these bodies, either as a member or as an observer, India's role as a leader gets fairly well established. It therefore has to ensure that it lives upto those expectations of the regional and global powers and showcases its capabilities to respond to various crises situations in the region.

Afghanistan

Islamist and extremist groups and the Talibans including Neo-Talibans in FATA, NWFP and Afghanistan make another cause for India to rise and respond to this new regional threat which has attracted the attention of entire world community. The latest developments in Afghanistan and the consequent outcome of Af-Pak policy will have a profound effect on the global as well as the regional security matrix. India has considerable security interests in Afghanistan and may have to spread its wings much more than what it has done in the past.

China

The country which India has to worry about most is China. It views India as a threat to its pre-eminence in Asia because of the latter's potential to compete with it for natural resources, geo-strategic dominance and socio-political influences in the region. It would like to deny India strategic space in Asia, Africa and Latin America and to see India confined to South Asia as a regional power. In such a relationship some tension will always be present. Moreover, China is feverishly upgrading its military forces and space capabilities. In 2007 it surprised the world by shooting down a satellite with a missile. Its military budget for the past ten years has been recording a double digit rise. Growing at this rate the Chinese armed forces will become a formidable machine. It is also developing a blue navy with nuclear submarines and aircraft carriers that will enable it to project power in distant seas like the Indian Ocean. Specially worrisome to India is the 'string of pearls' it is creating all around the sub continental India, a deep sea port at Gwadar off Baluchistan coast in Pakistan, a road from Yunnan in China to Bay of Bengal, surveillance facilities in islands of Myanmar and ports in Myanmar and Sri Lanka. It also has arms supply relationship with Nepal and Bangladesh.

Furthermore, China is unlikely to unravel the problems of borders in Arunachal Pradesh and Aksai Chin as it does not believe that a compromise will serve any of its purposes. It seems to be convinced that peacefully agreed border adjustments will not upset settled population in the disputed areas. The issues remain mired in procedures, far from substance. Numerous other similar developments have forced India to exercise restraint and caution in dealing with China. It had opposed India's access to Nuclear Supply Group in 2008 until forced by the US. On the Mumbai terrorist carnage by Pakistan, its scholars and media, all state controlled, expressed doubts about Pakistani complicity and placed the blame squarely on internal contradictions in India. Thrice China had blocked UN efforts to have Jamaat-ud-Dawa, the Pakistani organization behind the outrage, declared an international terrorist organization in 2006.

We therefore need to take note of the likely implications of China's military modernisation, improvement of infrastructure in Tibet Autonomous Region and other related issues which are likely to affect our security concerns in the long term. Our mutual economic ventures and prolonged diplomatic efforts at resolving the boundary issues are positive steps towards normalisation of our bilateral relations but we must make sure that we successfully assert ourselves in the region as a regional player and take adequate steps in that direction.

Pakistan

Relationship with Pakistan has always been intensely problematic. It has its roots from the partition days when Pakistan came into existence as a result of the two-nation theory. The genesis of the problem lies in Pakistani covetousness for the J&K state. Four wars have been fought between the two countries and the proxy war continues unabated for the past three decades. Single minded antagonism towards India has led to an environment of fear and suspicion in Pakistan since it appears to be having a single point agenda of opposing India in every aspect of bilateral or multilateral dialogue. The situation in Pakistan continues to remain as fluid as ever. Their obsession with Kashmir would continue to determine their politico – military policies. Their continued support, covert as well as overt, to the spread of religious fundamentalism globally and regionally, will continue to affect the security dimensions in the region. The developments in Pakistan in the backdrop of Af–Pak policy also need to be watched carefully over the next few years. These new developments have altered Pakistan's strategic objectives. The Pakistani state has greatly weakened over the past few years. A perceptible environment of instability, uncertainty and haze prevails throughout the country. A sizeable chunk of its North Western region has become Talibanised. Large sections of the security establishment including its intelligence and paramilitary forces subscribe to the Islamist ideology. The "Zia-bharti" group of officers and men in the defence and paramilitary forces are suspected to be working towards transformation from Islamism to Jihadism. As Talibanisation creeps into the hinterland and nearer to Islamabad and Rawalpindi the probability of the security establishment donning the colours of jihadism becomes somewhat real.

The jihadi aim is to set up India as an Islamic Caliphate. Unconfirmed inputs suggest that they are cultivating and counting on large sections of Indian muslims who would come forward and support them in their 'nefarious' jihad designs. Such designs, and the fact that the jihadis may have an access to its nuclear arsenal, make it one of the most dangerous spots in the world. Most intelligence agencies in the world are believed to have acknowledged, albeit informally, that if another 9/11 hits the world its source would be Pakistan who has provided refuge to the Al Qaeda leadership. All these factors cannot be ignored by India while carving its strategic aims and defining its various policies.

SAARC Countries

India's relationship with most of its immediate neighbours has not been very harmonious. This includes Nepal, Bangladesh, Myanmar and Sri Lanka. One of the possible reasons for this could be India's size as compared to that of the neighbours, which gives rise to misplaced suspicions amongst these nations about hegemonic aspirations on the part of India. However, the recent political developments in our immediate neighbourhood are a welcome change and will affect the security paradigms in the region. Transition of Nepal into a Republic, gradual shift from hereditary monarchy to a democratic order in Bhutan, establishment of a new democratically elected set up in Bangladesh and a near decimation of LTTE in Sri Lanka are some of the events that will define the contours of regional stability in this part of the world. Similarly, increased maritime activity in the IOR should raise our hackles since protection of our Island territories located far away from the main land would assume added significance and shall demand appropriate resource allocation to deal with various out of area contingencies.

Thus, there are multiple challenges for India in its neighborhood. The most obdurate challenge would remain terminating Pakistan's proxy war. Islamist and extremist groups and the Talibans including Neo Talibans in FATA, NWFP and Afghanistan, making a common cause can play a dominant role in destabilizing the entire South Asian region. Presence of a nuclear arsenal in Pakistan, and the fact that the fundamentalist can have an access to these arsenals, make the environment infinitely more dangerous. A whole galaxy of scenarios therefore is possible. The way ahead for India, thus, is not going to be smooth even as it most certainly rises to regional and global eminence. In view of these developments there is definitely an urgent need to raise and develop sizeable "air-mobile" and naval task forces which can be rapidly deployed in the 'areas of interest' and 'areas of influence'. Its naval power needs to be built to levels that would at least permit sea-denial, if not sea-control in the entire Indian Ocean Region (IOR). Such should be its force projection capabilities as would deter even major powers to venture or even attempt military coercion anywhere close to areas of influence. Declaratory Force Projection Doctrine must clearly spell out India's intents in terms of situations and templates that would force India to reach out with adequate force, to regional and sub-regional territories as and when it is convinced that it's geopolitical, socio-economic and territorial interests are challenged. It is to be made known, more by actions rather than mere announcements, that the defensive and reactive policies that have had a debilitating impact on India's military preparedness and strategic dimensions are a thing of the past. In future, as soon as the crisis emerges it will rise to the occasion and 'project' its intents in a convincing, nonchalant and an assertive manner. It is imperative therefore that our 'Force Projection' efforts are directed at developing our off-shore island territories and converting them into strong military bases that are capable of sustaining our forces for any and every Out of Area Contingency and Effect Based Operations.

Our defence policy and planning has to be based on collective defence forces' influence with optimum utilization and effect of military power and potential, and not on that of any individual service. It has to be acknowledged and accepted that synergy is the key to success and it can be ensured only when our war fighting aims, goals, resources and techniques are harmonized by a single doctrine.[5] Enhanced tri-service integration, suitably supported by political will, resonant bureaucracy and deft defence diplomacy is therefore the appropriate recipe for achieving palatable Force Projection options for the country.

Our defence forces should be capable of operating 'out-of-area' as part of an integrated task force, when ordered by Government. They should be optimally equipped and weaponised to operate effectively in an integrated environment over the entire spectrum of conflict in the regional context including out of area contingencies and force projection dimensions. India has to acknowledge that great powers define their vital national interests expansively. They delineate their defence parameters far from homeland on the shores of distant littorals and oceanic choke points. Moreover, by seeking to extend their military protection to an ever widening circle of countries they increase their legitimate sphere of influence. And they achieve all this by expanding a lot of political and military effort and, in the process, blood, sweat and riches. But the payoffs are huge[6]. In order to be counted in the group of such great nations, India will need to make certain doctrinal changes by 2020. Some of the recommended changes are:-

- Be strong in conventional, asymmetric and nuclear capabilities to strengthen its deterrent capability.

- Fight every war in future in an integrated manner.

- Ensure macro level restructuring of its forces to be able to thwart external and internal threats and to undertake out of area contingency operations.

---

[5] Gen (Retd) V P Malik, "Indian Defence Forces : Preparedness to Counter 21st Century Challenges", CLAWS Journal Winter 2008, p5

[6] http://www.india-seminar.com, Bharat Karnad, "Aim Low Hit Lower".

- Focus on force projection options to assert its rightful dominance in South Asia and Indian Ocean Region.

- Raise the bar for levels of technology in all its manifestations to add teeth to its defence forces.

- Accord adequate priority to Special Forces and coup-de-main forces who will play a crucial role in joint force projection options.

- Raise amphibious formations suitably grouped with other elements for consolidating the force   projection capabilities.

- Have adequate air lift capability for speedy insertion of the integrated force(s) in the intended area of operations, both within and away from the homeland.

These changes, and many more similar ones, have to be weighed in the backdrop of significant developments taking place in the global and regional scenario in our neighbourhood. Old issues persist while the new ones are added. The role of military power has increased as security concerns spread beyond national boundaries. There is a need to protect our core competencies, identify complementary capabilities in all defence and civil organizations, develop sound and effective interfaces and train to consolidate the concept of integration, jointness and synergy. The core competence of each of the elements of national power must be synergized to encourage inter- disciplinary integration. It's the synergized and capability based approach alone that can help the nation tackle security challenges in the new millennium. We have to understand that the warfare in this new millennium is changing rapidly due to the fluid and ever changing geo-strategic environment around the world. Politically, socio-economically and militarily weak nations are searching for asymmetric ways of contending with their powerful and dominant adversaries. Morals and ethics are being compromised and international relations are witnessing a new phenomenon where inordinate influence of personalities dictates the 'bonding and structures' of emerging alliances. Thus, the geo-political scenario around the world is changing fast and a new world order is bound to emerge. Where does India fit into this new order will depend upon its socio-economic, diplomatic, economic and military strength. The scourge of fundamentalist tendencies, belligerent neighbourhood, disturbed surroundings and uncertain political environment have to be factored into our strategic planning and policy guidelines.

India has to ensure that strength, sustainability, reliability and global reach of Indian Defence Forces should be built up and comprehensively strengthened to serve the political directives and national objectives in dealing with the force projection options for the country. It must ensure that its Comprehensive National Power (CNP) is so well amalgamated, blended and integrated that they are able to undertake all types of force projection tasks and assignments.

CHAPTER 2

ELEMENTS OF FORCE PROJECTION

Though force can protect in emergency; only justice, fairness, consideration and cooperation can finally lead men to the dawn of eternal peace.

- General Dwight D. Eisenhower

Last few decades have witnessed drastic changes in the global dynamics of security and strategy. The strategic comforts offered by national boundaries and territorial dimensions no longer constitute effective defence. Numerous regional fora have evolved to challenge the supremacy of any single power bloc. International cooperation has grown and a sense of global interdependence has emerged to tackle issues such as resurgence of hard core ideological fundamentalism, presence of weapons of mass destruction and the fear of their exploitation by subversive elements, oil diplomacy, inter and intra Arab disputes and hostilities, sea piracy etc. The nations are willing to step out of their territorial frontiers to address these issues not only in close proximity of their borders but anywhere and everywhere on the globe. They are willing to employ all elements of national power to respond to crises, to contribute to deterrence, to enhance global as well as regional security and to showcase their military might in pursuit of power projection.

In military and diplomatic calculations, projection of force is the capacity, either implied, or demonstrated in practice, to exert control over distant theatres through military action. Changes in a country's capacity to project force may have immediate consequences for diplomacy and international trade agreements. Thus, power projection or force projection depicts the ability of a nation to send its defence forces away from its territorial boundary in response to various types of crises, be it of military nature or during catastrophic disasters. This ability is a crucial element of a state's power in international relations. Traditionally speaking, this capability was primarily dependent on 'hard power' assets such as tanks, aircrafts, naval vessels, special forces etc. However, lately the concept of "soft power" suggests that the power projection does not necessarily entail deployment of defence forces.

It can equally be achieved by means of humanitarian assistance, disaster relief and aid to civil power at the times of crises and other similar situations. An effective and demonstrated power projection capability can promote security and deter the aggression of a belligerent power. Such a capability would call for execution of multiple, simultaneous, synergized, synchronized and well coordinated military operations in a real time frame.

Historically speaking, the concept of force projection is as old as the emergence of the concept of nation states. Right since the time 'societies' emerged as a collective group of men and women, they have indulged in collective defence of their tribes and wilful projection of their military might in varying degrees of capability, proficiency, sophistication and finesse. The 19th century is replete with examples of force projection such as the 1864 Bombardment of Kagoshima and the Boxer rebellion. Similarly, 20th century saw the Japanese demolition of the Imperial Russian Navy's fleet during the Russo – Japanese war of 1904-05. More recently, the Falkland War showed the United Kingdom's ability to project military force miles away from home. The war in Vietnam, Gulf War and Afghanistan are wars which fall under the category of force projection.Even the Maldives was a successful force projection demonstration by India.

Force Projection Consideration

Force Projection operations inherently imply that they, in all probability, will be multinational and may vary in duration for the participating nations. Force composition may include temporary alignment of countries for narrowly focused objectives, informal coalitions to provide for common action in accomplishing limited objectives, and long standing alliances. The longer a coalition is sustained, more are the opportunities offered to standardize and integrate tactics, drills, procedures and techniques amongst the participating forces.

Considering the nature of these operations, there is a need to identify certain key considerations that will have a direct bearing on the outcome of these operations. Some of these considerations have been listed below:-

Intelligence

Success of any Force Projection Operation, irrespective of the country that launches it, will depend upon accurate and real time detailed intelligence.   The flow of information therefore, must be continuous to ensure speedy collection, collation, interpretation and dissemination of actionable intelligence to the environment. The anticipatory information in terms of terrain, topographic details, climatic inputs etc must be compiled as a data bank and should be shared with all those forces and elements that are likely to participate in Force Projection Operations.

Force Composition

Deliberate thought will be needed to decide on the Force composition. Though the intended mission will dictate the final composition of the force required to be projected, there is a definite need to equip Task Forces with appropriate teeth and lethality in terms of manpower and equipment profile so as to achieve the desired force projection aim. Proper force composition will give the operational commander, the resources and the dispositions to deal with any and every eventuality that might jeopardize or compromise the mission of the force.

Training

Relevant training helps in building team spirit and facilitates the Task Force to focus on their mission. It also enables the participating troops to acquaint themselves with conditions that are expected to be found during force projection operations.

Command and Control Set Up

In view of the joint and possibly multinational nature of force projection operations, commanders need to establish a set up that can exercise effective command and control over the entire force. It should be flexible enough to meet the multi dimensional challenges that stare at such force projection outfits.

Logistic Support

Success in any force projection operation hinges on the fulcrum of sound logistic support. Effective utilization of existing infrastructure in terms of roads, railway lines, airfields, ports, water resources etc will have to be built into the logistic support plan. Requisite inputs on the availability of such logistic support in the intended area of operations must be obtained from the intelligence agencies.

Media Policy

Force Projection operations will always attract immense media attention. A sound media policy will therefore be needed to project the national aim and the intended mission and the Force Projection operations without any sensationalization. Various Defence Correspondents and analysts will have to be appropriately briefed to avoid speculative comments and incorrect derivations.

Elements of Force Projection

Integrated force projection is an advanced concept that demonstrates joint perspective. It empathizes with the nation's need to develop one single integrated force from end to end. This force may operate either independently, as was the case in Sri Lanka and Maldives operations, or as a part of the multinational force under an Overall Force Commander (OFC) as was done in the Gulf War and is currently being followed in Afghanistan. In either of these situations there is a requirement to have certain elements that would constitute each integrated force. While few long range weapons such as Inter Continental Ballistic Missiles (ICBMs) and some of the cruise missiles may contribute to force projection in their own way, they cannot be called the sole elements of force projection. More reliance will have to be laid on carrier battle groups, strategic bombers, ballistic missile submarines, nuclear powered submarines and strategic airlift capability. Airborne Special Forces with their strategic capabilities are the obvious elements of choice for all such operations. The ability to integrate naval and air forces with land forces, in all their dimensions, will play a decisive role in all such power projection ventures. Use of technology based communication network and net centric warfare capabilities are major force multipliers for all such task forces who may have to operate miles and miles away from the homeland.

Another significant element that cannot be ignored is the logistics. The huge cargo holds and inter continental flight capabilities are an inescapable prerequisite for conceiving all such force projection capability to simultaneously lift and apply all or some of the elements of national power – political, economic, strategic and military, to the intended area of operations. Post deployment, prolonged sustenance and speedy disengagement on culmination of operations should be made in detail.

The option of "forward basing" that allows pre-positioning and locating the force(s) in the vicinity of intended area of operations should also be weighed in terms of likely dividends vis-à-vis international opinion and reaction to such a pre-positioning of expeditionary force. This option will also have to take into account the national policy directive on strategic objectives desired to be achieved in the long run. Ideally speaking, this directive should emphasise on capacity building in terms of advance remote sensing capabilities, long range precision munitions, enhanced manoeuvre capabilities and rapid movement and deployment of the force projection platforms. Unambiguous and clear guidelines must be laid to stress the need for suitable training and preparation of the expeditionary forces to ensure their perennial preparedness for deployment in a zero-notice scenario. It may be even better to identify and earmark embarkation nodes with clear timelines that define the mobilisation parameters in terms of "lift off" and "sail out" time limits post issue of Warning Order.

As regards the universally important element of Industrial Base, it must be ensured that the shortfall in equipment and supplies must be made expeditiously so as to facilitate speedy deployment in the shortest time frame required for a "no-notice" or a "zero-notice" crisis scenario.

Lastly, the three most important and major elements of personnel readiness, logistics sustenance and sound training must always be kept as the uppermost consideration for meeting the demands and requirements of the National Security Strategy in pursuing the aims of Force Projection. Moreover, the expanded dimensions of security also necessitate a much closer interaction between various organs of the state, which were hitherto-fore divested from decision making matrix in the sphere of national defence. This integration can emanate from a joint organisational framework which can delve upon varied security threats, external as well as internal, and continuously evolve strategies to overcome their adverse impact; while at the same time, enlarge scope for enhancing national power in each sphere. It has been felt that as the field of security expands, inter agency coordination assumes greater importance. India's aspirations to be a power of consequence in the days ahead will thus be determined by the speed, flexibility and fidelity at which the instruments of state can integrate and interact with each other.[7] The elements of force projection will therefore have to mesh seamlessly to achieve a real time, surgical and precise application of the desired task force to confront the impending crisis or contingency.

---

[7] "India's Comprehensive National Power: Synergy Through Joint Decision Making – A Study Report" by CENJOWS, 2009, pp2

CHAPTER 3

OUT OF AREA CONTINGENCY OPERATIONS

Confront them with annihilation, and they will then survive; plunge them into a deadly situation, and they will then live. When people fall into danger, they are then able to strive for victory.

- Sun Tzu

The concept of force projection is as old as the concept of formation of nation states. In fact, it may not be incorrect to state that the former precedes the latter. Right from the primordial and pre-historic times when humans started getting together as a society, they have resorted to collective defence not only to ensure their territorial defence but also to conquer adjacent territories or to assist friendly kingdoms and countries in thwarting aggressive designs of the adversaries. Thus, in its rudimentary form, the concept of operating away from the homeland to address 'out of area contingencies' has been associated with the mankind since ages. Even today, most nation states nurture force projection aspirations and periodically test their extant-military capabilities to translate their desire into reality so as to effectively deal with various crisis situations. Unfortunately for India, the desire to reach out and send expeditionary forces for force projection has never been a part of its tradition. With immense indigenous wealth and rich natural resources, India never looked beyond the national frontiers to extend its strategic reach. This inertia, perhaps, is responsible for our insular look towards our security strategy.

This 'inertial mindset' changed when the Britishers arrived in the subcontinent and deployed expeditionary Indian Colonial troops overseas in various theatres of war and extended India's reach from the Suez Canal and Red Sea in the West to East China Sea in the East; and from Asiatic Russia and Central Asia in the North to Indian Ocean in the South.[8] Over the years India realised that a paradigm shift was needed to shed its presumptuous, egoistic and over confident mindset. It acknowledged that its geo-political landscape was volatile, challenging and susceptible to exploitation by external actors. It needed to carve out its strategic policies not in an insular manner but by considering the geo strategic interests of its neighbours, allies, enemies and neutrals and their individual as well as collective and collusive impact on our own security dynamics. Today there is a convergence of purpose among decision makers, politicians, diplomats, strategists, think tanks, academicians and almost amongst the entire country that India's emergence as a Regional Power necessitates that it asserts itself, convincingly and substantially, to undertake force projection operations whenever situation so demands. It must leverage the geo political space that is afforded by the peninsular landmass that dominantly juts into the Indian Ocean and extends the country's out of area reach primarily within the South Asian region and largely in other areas of the world to address numerous crisis situations.

A crisis is an incident or a situation that poses an internal or external threat to a nation, to its territorial integrity, to citizens, geo-political interests, and to vital areas and vital points. A crisis develops rapidly and creates a condition of such diplomatic, economic or military importance that the affected nation is forced to commit its national resources in terms of diplomatic forays, economic assistance and use of military might, if required. Such crisis can occur during peacetime, conflict or war. In peacetime a crisis can be precipitated

---

[8] Trishul, Vol XXI No 1 Autumn 2008, R Adm (Retd) Rakesh Chopra, VSM, PhD, "Strategic Capabilities in the New Millennium : Expeditionary Forces for Out of Area Contingency", p 33

by a natural disaster or civil disobedience resulting in a threat to civil authority. In war, the focus of threat can be directed at the sovereignty of a nation. The extent to which the defence forces are prepared to respond to a crisis will significantly influence the eventual outcome. These response options for the military, however, will have to be suitably backed by other instruments of national power such as economic, diplomatic and informational alternatives, all of which have to be applied synergistically.

As far as India is concerned it has to cater for the full spectrum of threat from Low Intensity Conflict Operations (LICO) and proxy wars to all out conventional and nuclear wars because of an environment of uncertainties as regards our immediate neighbours. Our response to external threats and challenges has always been of restraint, calculative, measured and moderate; consistent with our peaceful outlook and reputation as a non- aligned peace loving nation. This approach needs to change now. We need to redefine our goals and focus more on according utmost priority to our economic reforms and agenda. It's an era of globalisation and we must forge strategic partnership with some of the major players in the world. Whilst diplomacy must remain our foremost means of dealing with challenges related to security, there could be no worthwhile development without ensuring adequate security for the country. In other words, we need a strong military muscle and strategic capability. Therefore, it is essential that we clearly identify and define our National Security Strategy from which would flow our military strategy to safeguard our national interests and aspirations for recognition as a regional power. There is thus a pressing need for a clearly enunciated national strategic vision for the armed forces spanning over the next few decades. This strategic vision must define, loud and clear, our aims and objectives with regards to contingencies that may emerge not only within the confines of the territorial boundaries but also those which may come up miles and miles away and have a direct or indirect bearing on our geo-strategic environment and our rising status as a regional power. The operations fall into the ambit of Contingency Operations and need to be addressed differently than the methodology of a conventional war.

Contingency Operations

A contingency operation is the employment of national resources (such as politico-diplomatic instruments, military muscle, economic might, industrial and commercial assets etc) in response to a crisis caused by natural disasters, calamities, political coups, terrorist violence or even by some coercive action of a belligerent nation. A contingency could be a stand alone event or may be a part of certain well planned and executed operations or a series of operations. Due to the uncertainties and peculiarities of the situation they require meticulous planning, rapid response, and flawless execution —— all in a synergised realm of force application. For achieving a high degree of assured success probability through synergistic application, following key mobility initiatives would be essential:-

- Maritime capability that facilitates rapid deployment of the 'force projection' task force.

- Adequate airlift capability for speedy insertion of the force into the intended area of contingency operations.

- Infrastructural facilities to ensure ready platforms for concentration of the task force and its subsequent launch by sea or by air.

- Procedures and guidelines to requisition national assets and resources for efficient and speedy deployment of the task force.

Contingency operations would assume added significance in the foreseeable future because large scale wars are unlikely anymore. Future conflicts will be short duration conflicts limited in terms of time, force allocation, desired attrition and the ultimate objectives to be achieved. These operations will require a high degree of pre-emptive diplomacy, joint planning, surgical execution and an effective perception management. Military Commanders, in particular must understand and address the peculiar requirements that are critical for the successful outcome of such out of area contingency operations. While rapid deployment, prompt response and time sensitivity are critical pre requisites for the successful culmination of such operations, it is important that the characteristics associated with these operations are well understood and analysed. Some of these peculiar characteristics are listed below;-

- Sound and real time intelligence

- Aggressive intent

- Effective diplomacy

- Rapid force projection capability

- Well trained, rehearsed and synergised tri-service military component

- Effective communication network

- Credible theatre air and missile defence to provide adequate protection to the task force as well as to launch pads and lodgement areas.

Concept of Out of Area Contingency

Out of area operations encompass a wide range of activities in which primarily the military instrument of national power is used in ways other than the large scale conventional combat operations usually associated with war. Notwithstanding the small size of these force levels and scales of operations, they are meant to serve the strategic intent of the nation. These operations will follow a general sequence or a series of stages. Activities of one stage may blend with another, be parallel to another, or not occur at all.

Force Projection Stages

The force projection stages are not necessarily distinct or sequential, and therefore, pose immense planning and execution challenges for the commanders. Intelligence agencies and staff officers must be prepared to assist the commanders in meticulous planning, execution and monitoring of these operations. The following stages provide the general structure for a force projection operation:-

- Mobilisation

- Pre-deployment

- Deployment

- Entry Operations

- Main or Decisive Operations

- Conflict Termination and Post Conflict Operations

- Redeployment and Reconstitution

- Demobilisation

Stage 1: Mobilisation

Mobilisation is the process by which the armed forces or the earmarked force projection component is brought to a state of enhanced readiness for embarking upon the assigned contingency operation. This process of mobilisation permits augmentation of the task force in a pre planned, well rehearsed and time tested manner. Once mobilisation is ordered these forces may concentrate either at a single pre-determined rendezvous or at multiple launch pads. In either of these cases the finer aspects of tri-service and multi agency coordination are resolved and the command and control of all the components passes on to the designated Overall Force Commander who, thereafter, assumes the operational command of the Force Projection contingent.

Stage 2: Pre-deployment Activities

Pre-deployment activities provide the foundation for subsequent force projection operations. This is a critical stage of the contingency force projection operations during which units train, prepare and coordinate various issues that are essential for the success of the force projection operations. The objective in this phase is to select proper force composition and thereafter validate various operational concepts for the actual conduct of the force projection operations. Decisions made in this pre-deployment stage will have a direct bearing on integration, coordination and synergising of the task force into a well knit, cohesive and a credible force with adequately tested and honed up skills in dealing with various contingencies. Horizontal and vertical interaction must occur between commanders and their staff during this stage so that plans can be made concurrently. At this stage liberal decentralisation will pay rich dividends in achieving peerless coordination, nonpareil synthesis and consummate synergy. Mission accomplishment, to a large extent, will depend upon the successful conduct of various events during this stage. Therefore certain planning considerations are critical during this stage to ensure that the desired aims are achieved without any hindrances.

Most important consideration pertains to the extremely difficult aspect of collection of intelligence. Force Commanders define their intelligence requirements during this stage and make an endeavour to stay upfront in intelligence planning by developing broad baseline knowledge on contingency areas and to understand how to get intelligence support. Staff, during this stage, will continuously scan the environment, assess the challenges and identify opportunities that ought to be exploited during the actual conduct of the contingency operations. Other considerations include optimisation of communications, networking data and arranging latest satellite image maps and terrain analysis templates. Similarly, anticipatory logistics will have to be worked out to project support requirements and synchronize support actions with various tactical sub groups constituting the force projection operations.

Validation of load tables also needs to be carried out to ensure that combat power could be sustained or reconstituted as required. Last, and equally important, is the identification of potential consequences by commanders to see that the prioritisation is done in a manner that the earmarked force is fully prepared to deal with any and every contingency that may arise during the launch stage.

Stage 3: Deployment

Success of the force projection operations hinges primarily on the sea-lift and air-lift capabilities of a nation. The primary consideration therefore, in deciding on the appropriate composition of the projection force, will have to be weighed in the backdrop of availability of sea-lift and air-lift assets both, within the defence forces as well as from the trade and industry. Other crucial factors during the deployment stage will be the host nation's capability to provide appropriate operational and logistic support to the projection force. The commanders, during this stage, have to maintain a balance between speed in deployment of the task force and the protection that it enjoys through the host nation at the time of launch.

It is crucial for the Force Projection Commander to retain surprise, ensure flexibility in execution of plans and achieve concentration of force at the point of decision by generating superior combat power during this stage to ensure the success of the force projection operations.

Stage 4: Entry Operations

This constitutes the execution phase of the Out of Area Contingency Operations. The advance elements of the Projection Force and the forces of the host nation strive to build the intelligence picture to facilitate the main elements of projection force in launching their operations after due deliberations and modification of plans, wherever required. The intelligence staff attempts to identify all threats to arriving forces and assists the commanders in developing force protection measures so that the projection force is not imbalanced by the hostile elements immediately on arrival in the area of operations in the host country. The support also includes provision of access to departmental and joint intelligence databank of the host nation. It is at this stage that the intelligence reaches the 'cross-over point' where the tactical intelligence becomes the commander's primary concern. From here onwards he starts relying more and more on the contact intelligence and humint and reduces his focus on top driven national and theatre intelligence. This entry stage encompasses occupation of initial lodgements and footholds in the operational area. The principal focus at this stage remains on building combat power as quickly as possible while concurrently conducting initial operations to establish footholds in the intended area of operations. Particular attention is given to the build up of collective capability which is critical for conduct of sustained operations.

Stage 5: Main or Decisive Operations

Success of Entry Operations hinges on speedy application of combat power and on retaining initiative and flexibility. Coupled with this is the requirement of synergy between the force components and the host nation's forces. Careful synchronisation of all elements – land, sea and air, are crucially important during the critical execution phase. Commanders must try and seize unheld or unopposed pockets while simultaneously launching operations to brush aside minor oppositions and lightly held positions before they are reinforced by the opposing forces. Speed, high tempo, aggression and decentralisation are extremely important at this decisive stage of the contingency operations. Principle of Simultaneity is invoked to ensure that the hostile forces are engaged throughout the length, breadth and depth of the area of operations.

It is through these decisive combat operations that commanders of the Force Projection Task Force aim at achieving those objectives which have been assigned to them prior to launch of the Out of Area

Contingency Operations. It's only then that the politico-strategic aim of the campaign would be achieved.

Stage 6: War Termination or Post War Operations

Once the strategic aim of the operation is achieved its time for termination of the war i.e. the out of area contingency. Consolidation Operations therefore commence from this point onwards. This stage may commence even when the residual combat operations and the mopping up efforts are still under way.

These post conflict operations focus on restoring proper order, reconstruction of damaged and destroyed infrastructure and setting the stage for transition from war to peace. These operations comprise a number of activities that have political, economic and diplomatic implications. Most important of these activities is the clearance of minefields and removal of booby traps from the populated areas. This stage also entails launching of people friendly operations such as establishment of refugee camps, restoration of essential public services and utilities, reconstruction of damaged assets, rebuilding roads and bridges, provision of medical facilities, and above all, restoration of law and order. Confidence building measures assume added significance during this stage. Thus, this war termination stage has immense ramifications in furthering the strategic objectives of the projection force as well as the host nation.

Stage 7: Redeployment and Reconstruction

Redeployment and Reconstruction Stage takes care of the options for redeployment of the assets that were allocated to the projection force. The Force Commander has to ensure an optimum redeployment flow lest any residual components of the hostile forces exploit any weaknesses that may creep during the redeployment of the force components. The tendency to pull out all forces for demobilisation should be avoided. Care also needs to be taken while handing over the captured areas back to the host nation's forces to ensure that areas susceptible to any hostile action by residual hostile forces are held in adequate strength; and if needed, certain detachments of the projection force are left behind till situation stabilises fully.

Stage 8: Demobilisation

This is the stage in which the projection force plans to de-induct from the area of operations after having achieved the politico-strategic objectives assigned to it. However demobilisation and de-induction is also affected in a well planned and coordinated manner. The de-inducting force has to ensure that at no stage does it imbalance itself with respect to the tactical, operational and administrative capabilities. Its only when the de-mobilisation and de-induction is completed that the commander of the Task Force claims success for the Out of Area contingency Operations. Only then is the force projection mission considered to have been accomplished.

All these stages are invariably applicable to all those nations who are desirous of undertaking out of area contingency operations in pursuit of their global or regional aspirations, though of course, there will be few modifications to suit each one's operational, tactical and strategic concepts. However, in case of India, the very concept of incorporation of expeditionary forces into the military requires a doctrinal shift from an 'attrition mindset' to 'mission command' with 'decisive effect' by combining a defensive orientation of "dissuasion" with a proactive "offensive defence" strategy to maintain peace and deter conflict, thus achieving deterrence[9]. In this regard a pertinent point that merits attention is the dismal record of India in exploiting its geo-strategic location and the military power, primarily because, we as a nation, have been wary of exploiting our 'strengths'. The effects of these weaknesses are being felt now because scant attention is being given to India in recognition of its emerging power potential. It is merely being considered as a 'Key Global Player' whereas it should focus on acquiring the status of a 'Regional Power'

---

[9] ibid, pp36

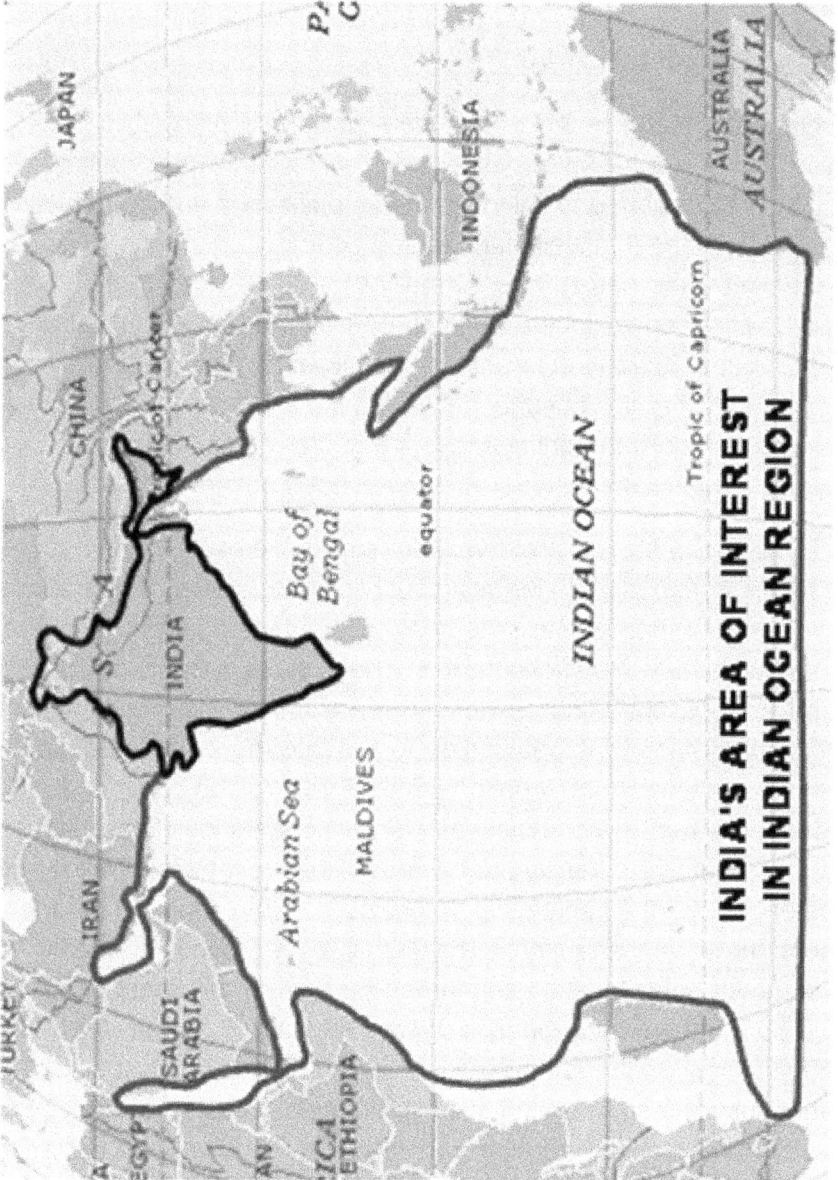

INDIA'S AREA OF INTEREST IN INDIAN OCEAN REGION

that aspires to become a 'Key Global Power' and shed the dubious tag of merely a 'Key Global Player' by the middle of this century. It should not stay content with the 'Strategic Attention' that it has got from the world community. Instead, it must claim 'Strategic Respect' that it rightfully deserves. This recognition will come its way only if it "demonstrates the will to use power and would do so unreservedly in pursuit of its national interest and objectives."[10]

It is imperative therefore that India projects its power through Out of Area Contingency Operations and Effect Based Operations. Even Kautilya, in Arthshastra, had stated that a state's power is greatest at home and declines along a "loss of gradient" as the distance from home to the 'rings' increases. This occurs because of the enhanced time and cost of transporting military resources. Expeditionary forces maintained for operations overseas prevent the loss of the 'strength gradient'. They constitute a latent threat and achieve 'operational deterrence' out of proportion to their size".[11] This viewpoint can easily be understood with the help of map showing the area of influence for India. India is singularly fortunate that its geo strategic location lends peerless advantages in terms of the domination of IOR region which affords immense potential for force projection operations in and around this region. Its vast coastline facilitates easy access to littoral regions and crucial choke points that have a direct influence on the flow of international trade through this region. The abundant space that is available for geopolitical manoeuvre should be exploited and leveraged to launch expeditionary forces for out of area contingencies with a view to stake its claim as a regional power.

---

[10] Paper No 2377, 17 Sep 2007, "India at Sixty – Strategic Reflections", DrSubhash Kapila, http://www.saag.org/common/uploaded_files/paper2377.html.

[11] Trishul, Vol XXI No 1 Autumn 2008, R Adm (Retd) Rakesh Chopra, VSM, PhD, "Strategic Capabilities in the New Millennium : Expeditionary Forces for Out of Area Contingency", p 35

Certain recommendations that merit attention of the policy makers, therefore, need to be made to help think tanks and strategists to evaluate them and decide on their implementation for furthering the cause of the nation in attaining a regional power status. These recommendations are:-

- Formulate Force Projection strategy based on following elements:-

  - Peacetime presence

  - Rapid crisis response

  - Forward deployment

  - Adequate logistic balance

  - Sustained politico-military pressure in area

- Resounding diplomatic signals to achieve political objectives

- Imaginative deception plan

- Evolve a sound synergised intelligence network that would encompass all intelligence agencies

- Force restructuring with emphasis on amphibious and air lift capabilities

- Exceptional degree of operational coherence and unity of effort

- Evolve a concept of Integrated Force Command as against the option of Overall Force Commander(OFC) adopted during the IPKF operations in Sri Lanka

The complexity of out of area contingency demands an exceptional degree of synergy, cohesiveness and unity of effort. Therefore, the force capability in our case must be enhanced considerably in terms of balanced amphibious and airborne components capable of 'rapid response' in 'zero-notice' environment that characterises such contingencies as military coups, terror strikes, humanitarian assistance, disaster management etc. Emphasis will have to be laid on resolution of contradictions between 'function oriented' and 'output oriented' systems of command and control of such a task force duly supported by C4I2SR and Network Centric Warfare (NCW) modules. Success of Out of Area Contingencies and Effect Based Operations (EBO) will always demand lubricating friction between inter agency rivalries and overcoming inertia in acknowledging other service's operational capabilities. This can only be achieved if a Unified Command and Control structure is established at the apex level with an exceptional degree of cohesion amongst all elements of Comprehensive National Power which will assist in delivering an encyclopaedic 'integrated effect' at the point of decision.

CHAPTER 4

EFFECT BASED OPERATIONS

"War is not merely an act of policy but a true political instrument, a continuation of political intercourse carried on with other means. The political object is the goal, war is the means of reaching it, and means can never be considered in isolation from their purpose."

- Carl von Clausewitz

Strategic planning has always linked military operations to a political outcome that is desired to be achieved by a nation. Thus, the barometer of success in any war or campaign has always been the political objectives and the extent to which these objectives have been achieved. Military power merely serves as one of the components of the Comprehensive National Power and contributes its might in speedy achievement of the politico-strategic aim of the war. Therefore, it is of important salience for the military leaders to understand that wars are not mere clashes between warring factions. They, in fact, are the highest form of struggle for resolving contradictions between classes, clans, nations, states and political groups, and have existed ever since the emergence of societal concepts of living. The laws of war therefore must be studied by the military leaders in great detail, moreso, because "different laws for directing different wars are determined by the different circumstances of those wars - differences in their time, place and nature. As regards the time factor, both war and its laws develop; each historical stage has its special characteristics, and hence the laws of war in each historical stage have their special characteristics and cannot be mechanically applied in another stage."[12] In fact the concept of war fighting goes through a phylogenic process and keeps evolving with changing times to match the contemporary transformations, pace by pace.

Effect Based Operations (EBO) is one such concept that has emerged in recent times, perhaps in the post cold war era. This concept apparently aims at addressing the newer threats that have mushroomed in the form of Irregular Warfare or the Fourth Generation Warfare (FGW). This FGW is fought in a different dimension of 'effect based operations' rather than the destruction centric, attrition based linear concept of Third Generation Warfare which aimed at matching the capabilities of the adversary, force by force, and relied heavily on mass rather than the momentum. EBO focuses on the desired end state and achieves its aim by creating an effect on enemy through a synergistic and collusive application of all elements of Comprehensive National Power which include political, diplomatic, economic and military components. Thus, full range of nation's military and non military capabilities are employed at all levels of operations namely strategic, tactical and operational levels. EBOs ensure that tactical and operational actions are explicitly a part of the strategic plan developed to achieve specific political results. It obviated the necessity of prolonged military campaigns, hither to fore undertaken merely to achieve destruction. Economy of effort, thus, automatically becomes implicit in the EBO concept. This concept requires a deep understanding of the political context of a conflict or contingency so as to facilitate the decision makers (political masters) and the implementers (military leaders) and all elements of Comprehensive National Power to foresee various consequences that would emerge once their plans are translated into action. Thus, the concept entails a broader outlook that does not rely merely on

---

12   Mao Tse Tung on War, First Edition 2008, Understanding War, p5

the military might of nation. It incorporates all the applicable elements of national power namely diplomatic, economic, military and informational for a given situation and is relevant across the entire range of operations. The strength of these EBOs lies in synergy amongst all stake holders, strong risk taking ability, truism, force structure that encourages cross pollination of ideas and methods of execution of operations, clarity of intent, uninterrupted flow of information and sound decision making ability of the commanders with suitable backing of the decision makers. Therefore, these Effect Based Operations 'provide a powerful, unifying and holistic conceptual methodology that commanders and staff can apply to all operations across the spectrum of conflict.'[13]

Main Features of Effect Based Operations

It may be appropriate to summarise the main features of Effect Based Operations to facilitate easy comprehension of the entire concept. These features are :-

- **Application of Comprehensive National Power (CNP)**

  The quiddity of the concept lies in synergistic application of the CNP as against the practice of piecemeal, sporadic and fragmented response by various components of the task force. The concept applies equally during war and peace when the nations are required to respond to disasters, calamities, instability, military coup etc.

- **Reliance on Effects**

  The concept places reliance on 'effects'. The emphasis shifts from attrition warfare to 'end results'. Thus, this concept tries and shortens the combat.

---

[13] Lt Col Allen W Batschelet, US Army, 'Effect Based Operations – A New Operational Model, http://www.iwar.org.uk/military/resources/effect-based-ops/ebo.pdf

- **Focus on Decision Superiority**

  'Decision' remains the core component of the Effect Based Operations. Commanders strive to achieve decision superiority through effective adaptation of the OODA loop.

- **Speedy Intelligence Build up**

  Like all other operations of war (OOW), intelligence plays a crucial and dominant role in the outcome of EBOs. Continuous and real time flow of actionable intelligence is critically pivotal for the successful outcome of any EBO campaign. Sound intelligence build up invariably hinges on the under mentioned factors :-

  - **Geographical Inputs**

    Information regarding the geographical coordinates of the intended area of the EBOs, surrounding geographical features, distribution of military and non military assets of the opponent within the physical battle space, location of sensors, weapon systems etc are some of the key issues that constitute geographical inputs and are vital for the success of EBOs.

  - **Socio Political Inputs**

    Information concerning social structures and prevailing political set up in the country where these operations are being planned will always be crucial. Commanders must have the knowledge about the populace; their inclination towards any particular group or political set up; socio political data; explicit political affiliations within the global geo political dynamics and other similar inputs that will have a direct bearing on the operations of the EBO Task Force.

- **Technical Data**

    Technical details about the adversary's force capabilities are equally important for a credible intelligence build up. Such information will have to be built up continuously for all those areas which fall into the ambit of perspective EBO targets.

- **Economic Setup**

    Inputs regarding economic setup in the target country to include industrial strength and infrastructural back up also need to be collated and analysed as an ongoing process.

- **Perception Management**

    Successful outcome of any EBO will depend, to a large extent, on perception management. The perception will have to be shaped up for the under mentioned domains:-

    - Within the home country

    - Inside the target country/area

    - Amongst the world community

- **Media Handling**

    Media plays a crucial role in moulding the perceptions and therefore dedicated efforts will have to be allocated to ensure that it contributes positively towards achieving a favourable degree of perception management by achieving a psychological dominance over adversary.

- **Centre of Gravity**

    One of the most important features of EBO is to identify and determine the adversary's centre of gravity (CG). "Centres of Gravity are those characteristics, capabilities or localities from which a military derives its freedom of action, physical strength or will to fight."[14] These CGs could be military establishments, infrastructure, power nodes, population centres or even the leadership itself. Thus the CG need not only be physical but could well be a philosophical imponderable that can impact the outcome of operations, subtly and tenuously.

The EBO perspective therefore "supports operational design by enhancing elements such as centres of gravity, lines of operations and decisive points. This allows commanders and their staff to consider a broader set of options to focus limited resources, creates desired effects, avoid undesired effects and achieve objectives."[15]

Challenges for Effect Based Operations

There is a need to understand that one has to fundamentally think and identify challenges that will have to be overcome for ensuring a successful outcome of any Effect Based Operation. These challenges, if not addressed in time, will continue to grow at an ever increasing pace, thereby retarding the momentum of the Effect Based Operations in an operational paradigm that couples the use of military force with purposeful political dimension that aims to achieve the most desirable political outcome within the framework of a pre-defined strategic objective.

Some of the challenges that need to be addressed by the EBO Task Force are:-

---

[14] http://www.afrlhorizons.com/briefs/Jun01/IF00015.html "Effect Based Operations: Application of New Concepts, Tactics and Software Tools that Support the Air Force Vision for Effect Based Operations."

[15] Joint Staff 17 Joint Doctrine and Education Division Staff, "Effect Based Thinking in Joint Doctrine", Leadership/Military Leadership, Issue 2nd Quarter 2009, p 60.

- Need to have an in depth knowledge not only of the adversary's capability but also of the friendly forces' participating in the intended operation.

- Clandestine and discreet collection of information.

- Deep understanding of the political and diplomatic context of the impending operation.

- Close cooperation with other international actors.

- Sound inter agency and intra agency coordination to overcome parochialism.

- Arrangements to incorporate Non Governmental Organisations (NGOs), Humanitarian Relief Groups and Volunteer Forces into overall plan.

- Sources of funding the operations and more importantly, sustaining it for longer duration, if the situation so demands.

- Modalities for stabilisation and reconstruction.

- Building in regular feedback mechanism.

- Establishing linkages between actions and effects; and incorporating them in joint training prior to launch.

- Enabling methodology for ensuring a favourable perception management.

Relevance of EBO Concept to India

After having disappointed itself for decades, India is now on the verge of becoming a great power. In the coming years it will have numerous opportunities to influence the geo-political spectrum and critical issues affecting the global as well as the regional security. It will emerge as an undisputed and unparalleled regional power by 2020, and its growth along with China and Russia may "form a de-facto geo -

strategic alliance to counter balance US and Western influence."[16] The world community has taken note of India's arrival in the power dynamics with powerful and sound economy, multi-ethnic and vibrant democracy, secular and multi religious society and above all a stable and established regional player that has the potential to make positive contributions in the global power equation.

In the backdrop of this recognition, India will have to carve out the contours of its grand strategy in a manner that it looks beyond the immediate borders and expands its reach to the extended neighbourhood that encompasses its littoral territory, IOR Region, Asian periphery, parts of the African continent as well as certain other regions of the globe that affect its interests. To achieve that objective, India will have to be prepared, at all times, to undertake effect based operations at a short notice, either on a collaborative platform or as a 'stand-alone' player. The concept of EBO therefore, will be as much relevant to India as to any other aspirant who aims to acquire the status of global or regional power. We have to work towards integration of several components of Comprehensive National Power which is a sine qua non of EBO. This would entail overcoming various challenges, evolving new doctrines, developing new concepts, reorientation in thought and action; and above all, an integrated joint approach.

Following recommendations are therefore made to initiate steps that will help us to adapt to the EBO concept which will be essential for our future strategic calculus:

• **Revitalised Intelligence Setup**

A plethora of intelligence agencies are operating in the country — each with its own work culture, ethos and charter of duties. All these set ups are running parallel to each other with no

---

16   TV Parsuram in Washington; Dec 06,2003; "India to Emerge as a Major Regional Power by 2015 : Report"

convergence whatsoever. Each one of them is working independent of the other with no intentions or inclinations towards having a collaborative set up. There is a strong need to enmesh these intelligence agencies into a well knit and frictionless entity that would effectively coordinate all their activities. Besides achieving this cohesiveness, massive technological impetus will have to be provided to this set up in terms of equipping them with latest sensors, electronic equipment and space based platforms. This institutionalised apparatus should be directly under the Cabinet Secretariat or the NSC with arrangements for speedy dissemination of information to all agencies in a 'real time' dimension.

- **National Command Post**

    The present system of having an Interim National Command Post (INCP) at Headquarters Integrated Defence Staff (IDS) should be formally adopted after due validation. It should graduate from a mere INCP to a fully operational National Command Post that should be manned 24 x 7 so as to respond promptly to any crisis. It should have two to three Crises Management Groups (CMGs) that could look after the Continental Contingencies, Maritime Contingencies and Disaster Management Cell(s). The staff at these NCP and CMGs must comprise representation from Ministry of Home Affairs (MHA), Ministry of External Affairs (MEA), Ministry of Defence (MoD), Ministry of Finance (MoF), Defence Forces, Research and Analysis Wing (RAW), Intelligence Bureau (IB) etc.

- **Integrated Force Structure**

    Synergy and jointness amongst the three defence forces may be an important factor but it cannot be the sole consideration for achieving integration. Therefore an integrated force structure will have to be evolved to include representation from all elements that constitute Comprehensive National Power. Such integration will ensure requisite redundancy at various levels of command and control set up as well as a sound logistic back up based on national capabilities and not on any service specific agency.

- **Strategic Alliances**

  Force Projection is an option that would invariably invite opportunities for strategic alliances since it would be difficult to come across contingencies where a nation would be allowed to undertake EBOs in a stand alone mode. Collaborative and collusive plans will have to be made for which strategic alliances would have to be worked out. Diplomatic forays therefore must afford anticipatory options which need to be inked by various alliance partners much before any contingency arises.

- **Training and Doctrine**

  The existent Joint Services Doctrine, as also the training directives focus only on the tri-service concept with no, or very little emphasis, on incorporating other elements of Comprehensive National Power. Political directives and guidelines may have to be issued to revise these doctrines with terms of reference that all elements of Comprehensive National Power, including public and private sector players, must be included to leverage the nation's strength for providing the requisite strategic punch.

- **Network Centric Capability**

  In order to adapt to concept of Network Centric Warfare (NCW) we need rapid induction of space based assets, UAVs, Early Warning Airborne platforms and sophisticated ELINT, COMINT and HUMINT capabilities, all of which will pay rich dividends for successful outcome of any EBO.

It can be conclusively stated that EBO is a concept that is going to stay. It is one capability without which a nation will not be able to project its force in a manner that gives it recognition as a Global or a Regional Power. India, with recent transformation as an emerging economic and military power, is fully competent to enter the select group of nations who have the potential to undertake EBOs and project their force with conviction to achieve the status of a Regional Power. We must consolidate our capabilities in this regard to cement our legitimate claim as a Regional Power that is well on course to be christened as a Global Power in the latter half of this century.

CHAPTER 5

FORCE PROJECTION BY OTHER COUNTRIES

Build me a son, O Lord, who will be strong enough to know when he is weak, and brave enough to face himself when he is afraid, one who will be proud and unbending in honest defeat, and humble and gentle in victory.

- Douglas MacArthur

CHINA

Any study on strategic issues conducted in India will remain incomplete if one does not factor-in the developments in countries like China, Pakistan, US and certain developed nations. Therefore, before dwelling on force projection options for India it would be pertinent to discuss the force projection models, policies and options being adopted by some of these nations.

As far as China is concerned a curious but important characteristic of Indo-China relations is the existence of asymmetric perceptions of mutual threat between these two nations. India tends to be deeply apprehensive regarding China; whereas China believes in underplaying any perceived threat from India. This asymmetrical threat perception leads to numerous speculations in diplomatic parlance, as well as in military planning, both of which have long-term implications on strategic dimensions in the region.

Today, China's military modernization is openly being talked world over. It is definitely on an ascendant trajectory, and perhaps, aims at adding military muscle to its flourishingly burgeoning economic and political clout so as to enhance China's national aspirations to emerge as a key global power by 2025. This military modernization is not occurring in a vacuum, nor can it merely be linked to her national aspirations. It arises from the threat perceptions that have been analysed by it (China) over the latter half of the 20th Century when the United States remained the pre-dominant power in Asia-Pacific consequent to disintegration of the erstwhile USSR. China, emerging as a Communist monolith in 1949 was the first one (besides USSR as the other pole of the bipolar world) to put the United States 'on notice' in 1950 with her entry in the Korean War conveying that American power in the Pacific would henceforth be challenged by China directly or by proxy[17]. Since its infancy, China has constantly, but directly, been promoting its strategic interests in the backdrop of the perceived threat perceptions listed below:-

- Geographically, China is a vast expanse of landmass that extends from Pacific Ocean in the East to the Eurasian heartland in the West. It has a coastline of almost 14,500 km and shares land frontiers with 15 nations. Thus, the geo dynamics alone poses immense challenge to its national security and sovereignty.

- China's economic prosperity zones lie along the coastal region thereby making them vulnerable and susceptible to external threat through naval forays.

- The sole super-power, the United States, has adequate presence in the Pacific and is reasonably well disposed towards China. Coupled with this is the chemistry between the US and Japan, which affords the former, tremendous

---

[17] http://www.saag.org/common/uploaded files/paper 2228.html; 01 May 2007

advantage in the form of a military ally located so close to China, especially to the economic zone on East Coast.

- Chinese apprehensions and fears that its peripheral "provinces" of Tibet and Xinjiang may be exploited by adversaries to engineer trouble in the Chinese heartland and destabilize its aspirations at becoming a global power.

- Taiwan, as always, continues to be a flash point and irritant for China and its international relations.

- Littoral aspirations and the need to thwart strategic threat through international waters is another major cause of concern.

- Eastward creep of NATO's enlargements towards Russia and subsequently towards Central Asian Republics (CAR) serves as an Appendix to the "possible plan" of encircling and containing China.

- Capability of the US and its allies to undertake following military operations against China so as to dwarf its rise as an emerging power also force China to adopt a pro-active stance in its geo-strategic calculus:-

  - Extensive cruise missile strikes against Strategic assets and major population centers/economic zones

  - Naval blockades to prevent free economic activity

  - Target China's littoral interests

  - Destruction of China's nuclear installations and arsenal

  - Space Warfare

  - Military intervention and overt or covert support to secessionist and fundamentalist movements in Xinxiang province

- Clandestine support to Tibet and Taiwan

China, apparently, is one of the very few nations to have assiduously studied and analyzed the strategic developments such as US invasion of Iraq, military intervention in Yugoslavia, the break up of erstwhile USSR and most recently, the ongoing US 'War against terror" in Afghanistan. Numerous National Defence White papers and doctrines are being studied and revised by the Chinese strategists and think tanks with immense investment in terms of Revolution in Military Affairs (RMA), acquisition of military hardware, venturing into the domain of space and cyber warfare and validating its plans for force projection by way of conducting series of exercises. War games titled "Stride-2009" launched in July 2009 by the People's Liberation Army (PLA) were a step in this direction and have certainly raised the hackles of some of the advanced countries, as also of its neighbours. It was for the first time that forces from the four major regional military commands stationed in the cities of Shenyang, Lanzhou, Jinan and Guangzhou were engaged in live-fire drills at distances of almost 1200-1500 kms from their bases. Earlier, such exercises were reportedly conducted by troops under a single military command. Thus, the analysts feel that the purpose of such exercises with troops could be to refine and test the 'command and control' system for the PLA's long range force projection capabilities that would necessitate rapid deployment of troops at longer distances.

China's regional rivals are increasingly uncomfortable with such measures that project the growing military prowess of China. It's a cause of worry for us in India because the Chinese ambitions of gaining access to some of the ports and airfields in the South China Sea, Indian Ocean and the Persian Gulf to pursue its so called strategy of "Strings of Pearl" will jeopardize India's strategic aspirations besides having a direct bearing on its national security.[18]

---

[18] Kent Ewing, China's War Games Un-nerve Neighbours; Aug 18, 2009 on www.centurychina.com/plaboard/posts/3852790.shtml

Indicators of China's Force Projection Intentions

A few decades ago Den Xiaoping had stated, "When our country is developed and more prosperous, we shall have a bigger role to play in the world".[19] Today the validity of this statement is getting ratified without any dispute as would be seen from some of the indicators elaborated in succeeding paragraphs.

- On 06 January 2009, a Chinese Naval Fleet arrived in the Gulf of Aden off the Somalian coast. It was carrying out the first escort mission against pirates – a task which was not undertaken by China hitherto fore. By 18 February 2009, the fleet completed twenty-one escort missions and demonstrated its growing naval capabilities as well as intentions of projecting itself far-away from the mainland. The fleet escorted ten Chinese merchant vessels and three foreign ones namely 'Hermione' from Germany, 'Viking Crux' from Singapore and 'Princess Nataly' from Cyprus. The fleet carried about 800 crew members including 70 soldiers from the Navy's Special Force and was equipped with ship-borne missiles and light weapons[20].

- Over the past few years China has gained adequate experience in long distance force projection through naval force deployment. This has accrued as a dividend consequent to numerous joint multi-nation exercises and military exchanges pursued by China over the last couple of years. Even during its escort mission to Somalia, China had entered the Indian Ocean through the Malacca straits clearly demonstrating its logistics prowess by refueling the two destroyers using its supply ship Weishanhu. This refueling capability certainly strengthens its force projection options.

---

[19] S Rajasimman, China's Naval Force Projection off Somalia, www.idsa.in/publications/stratcomments/S Rajasimman 020309.htm

[20] ibid

• China's Vice Foreign Minister addressed the United Nations on 16 December 2008 and said, "China is seriously considering naval ships to the Gulf of Aden and waters off the Somali Coast for escorting operations in the near future". This assertive statement amply indicates that China does not believe in hiding its intentions of projecting itself and has enough power and potential to kineticize its strategic interests overtly and openly in full international view and by adequately fore-warning the world community.

• Another important indicator of rise in China's status and stature at projecting its force world-over has been through its contributions to UN Peace Keeping Missions. For a country that became one of the permanent members of UN Security Council only in 1971; for a nation that sent its first batch of UN observers as late as 1989 and for a state that was condemned world-over for Tiananmen incident; it is indeed creditable to be the second largest contributor (amongst the permanent members) to the UN peace keeping missions.

• China's recent economic development and a virtually 'defiant and confrontationist' counter to US dominance has not gone un-noticed. The recent stand-off at Copenhagen World Summit sent clear signals that China has the 'will' and the 'potential' to project itself and 'defend' its strategic interests. The world community has certainly taken note of the Dragon's force projection forays in almost every field that affects the global fraternity.

China's Military Modernization and Force Projection Designs

China's National Defence White Paper released in Jan 2009 had hinted at Beijing's growing confidence on the world stage while showing firm commitment to further military modernization that would certainly enhance its force projection capabilities. One of the

Pentagon reports has also claimed that China is building an expanded military with a force projection far beyond its homeland.

China's long term comprehensive transformation of its military forces is improving its capacity for force projection and strengthens its anti-access and area denial capabilities. Consistent with a 'near term' focus on preparing for Taiwan Strait contingency, China deploys many of its most advanced systems to the military regions opposite Taiwan. It describes operating under "informatised conditions and improving integrated joint operations capabilities" as the primary objective for the PLA's build-up. Incidentally "Integrated Joint Operations" is the PLA's term for multi service, combined arms operations[21].

China, of late, is believed to have improved its C4ISR capabilities (Command, control, communications, computers, intelligence, surveillance and reconnaissance) through integrative technology. It is learnt that an "integrated military information network" came into operation in 2006 in China and that PLA was building "digital campuses" at its military academies. Communication between units and command centres is also benefiting from China's Beidou Global Navigation Satellite System (BGNS) which is likely to achieve full global coverage by 2015. If true, it would mean enhanced power projection capability for the PLA even though it (BGNS System) is believed to be inferior to America's well established Global Positioning System (GPS) technology. China also expects to lay a solid foundation for informationisation of the military by 2010; to make major progress by 2020; and 'by and large' reach the goal of informationisation by mid-century[22].

---

[21] Annual Report to Congress, Military Power of the People's Republic of China 2008, Chapter one – Key developments.

[22] Owen Fletcher, 'A Peak Into China's Military Mind ', Asia Times, Jan 2009

As per one of the United States analysis, China's military modernization has been planned in three phases as under:[23]

- **Phase I (Until 2010)**

    - **Aim:** To reduce military differential with world's major powers and build capability to contain likely adversaries and fight local wars successfully.

    - **Emphasis:** Emphasis would be to produce leaner and military machine by downsizing, restructuring and reorganizing force structures for modern warfare. It has already been moving in this direction and is likely to meet the deadline of 2010 that it had apparently carved out for itself.

- **Phase II (Until 2020)**

    - **Aim:** China to emerge as the regions predominant military power. Capabilities to be designed to uphold China's regional geo-political interests even militarily, if required.

    - **Emphasis:** Added emphasis would be laid to modernize People's Liberation Army's Navy (PLAN) and People's Liberation Army's Air Force (PLAAF). China is well on course to revamp its maritime forces and provide added strategic range and teeth to its air force, thereby consolidating its force projection capability.

- **Phase III (By 2050)**

    - **Aim:** Transform China into a world class military power.

---

[23] Dr Subhash Kapila,'China's Military Modernisation: Major Thrust Areas';http://www.saag.org/common/uploadedfiles/paper2228.html

- **Emphasis:** China is likely to focus on space and cyber space, nuclear deterrence and force projection capabilities to match leading global military powers.

Thus, over the past two or three decades world has witnessed a resurgent China seemingly unhappy with single power dominance – taking long and steady strides towards becoming one of the world's super powers.[24] It has not only focused on its economy, its military also has been growing from strength to strength making noticeable progress in all spheres of warfare that contribute towards enhancement of force projection capabilities. Its modernization plans explained above amply highlight its ambitions of announcing its arrival in the global power dynamics. Having third largest armed forces in the world and being the only Asian Power that has strategic assets which have a reach upto the Continental United States (CONUS), China has rightfully focused attention on developing its power projection capabilities as would be obvious from the following developments in China's military build-up:-

- With a vast expanse of territory to safeguard and also to enhance her projection capabilities China has focused heavily on creation of sizeable Rapid Reaction and Rapid Deployment Forces. The available details suggest the following capabilities:-

  - **Rapid Reaction Force (RRF)**

    - Air Mobile and sea-mobile forces equipped with light weapons for rapid reaction.

    - RRF can be applied within 10 hours anywhere on China's periphery.

---

[24] Sanjay Kumar, Asymmetric Capabilities of China's Military.

- It comprises one Airborne Corps, ten Infantry Divisions, Special Forces Battalions and Naval Infantry.

- Total strength of RRF is stated to be 2,85,000.

- **Rapid Deployment Force (RDF)**

  - Provide Second Assault Wave to RRF.

  - Can be deployed in designated areas within two to six days.

  - Strength comprises two Armies from Beijing and Shenyang Military Districts.[25]

- China has the most active Ballistic and Cruise Missile Program in the world. It has developed the capability to support its expeditionary forces from the mainland itself.

- China is developing a multi-dimensional program to limit or prevent the use of space-based assets by its potential adversaries during times of conflict or international crisis.

- It views outer space as far more than just another asset to be pursued in competition with others. Satellites play an important role in China's ambitions for globalization, commerce, finance and continued economic development. On the security front, China has long understood the centrality of space for military power in terms of service integration, force enhancement and force projection.[26] Having carried out a successful ASAT (Anti Satellite Weapon System) test in Jan 2007, it is reported to be pursuing the following in terms of space warfare capabilities to enhance its strategic reach:-

---

[25] ibid

[26] Eric D Hagt, "News Frontier in Sino-US Relations: Challenges in Space".

- Anti-Satellite Satellites

- Pulse Weapons

- Orbiting Laser and Beam Weapons

- Space mines.

- In 2009, numerous computer networks around the world, including those owned by the US government were subject to intrusions that appear to have originated from China. Such Cyber warfare capabilities can be gainfully exploited during OOA contingencies and EBO operations to target the host countries command and control set up.

Capabilities of PLAN

China's naval expansion has been under way for almost two decades now. Its naval forces "include 74 principal combatants, 57 attack submarines, 55 medium and heavy amphibious ships and 49 coastal missile patrol crafts".[27] Each one of its amphibious ships can carry a battalion of infantry (marines) and a tank squadron.

China, for long, had denied any plans to construct aircraft carriers. However, it is now evidently clear that it has an active aircraft carrier research and design program. It has already embarked on construction of three aircraft carriers which will be the mainstay of the three proposed Aircraft Carrier Groups that would comprise:-

- Aircraft Carrier with 40 SU-27 fighters on board

- Six to eight surface warships

- Two to three nuclear attack submarines

- Two auxiliary vessels

---

[27] http://www.globalsecurity.org/military/Library/report/2008/2008-prc-military.power01.htm

The PLA Navy is also improving its Over the Horizon (OTH) targeting capability with Sky Wave and Surface Wave OTH radars and is developing missiles with improved range and accuracy. It has received seven new domestically produced surface combatants in the past two years including II-class (Type 052C) DDGs fitted with the indigenous HHQ-9 long range Surface-to-Air Missile (SAM), two LUZHOU class (Type 051C) DDGs equipped with the Russian SA-N-20 long range SAM and three JIANKAI II-Class (Type 054 A) guided missile frigates (FFG) to be fitted with the medium range HHQ-16 vertically launch naval SAM currently under development[28]. These ships reflect leadership's priority on advanced anti air warfare capabilities which are so vital for all the force projection operations involving maritime forces. It has thus been laying adequate emphasis to improve its capabilities to conduct amphibious and airborne operations within the region and is believed to have deployed a brigade sized marine force co-located with the South Sea Fleet near Zhanjiang which is equipped with amphibious tanks and armoured personal carriers for an amphibious landing. China's fleet of amphibious vessels conducts modest size training exercises in coastal regions. Although China possibly has never conducted a division-scale or larger amphibious exercise fully coordinated with air support and airborne operations, its amphibious force is believed to be capable of landing at least one infantry division on a beach. If China were to use its merchant fleet, its capacity to move forces would increase, although inadequate air defence and lack of ability and training in cross-beach movement of forces would be crucial shortcomings. It is also believed to have built several air-cushion vehicles and evaluated their designs to suit their use by its amphibious force. Acquisition of a small number of these aircrafts will enhance rapid infantry assault capability of the expeditionary force and provide a viable option for China to undertake force projection operations in the region.

---

[28] Annual Report to Congress, Military Power of the Peoples' Republic of China 2008, Chapter One: Key Developments.

The above plans, therefore, would significantly alter naval balance in the Pacific and Indian Oceans and would strengthen and bolster China's force projection capabilities.

Capabilities of PLAAF

China continues to invest heavily in its military, particularly in its strategic arsenal and capabilities designed to improve its ability to project power beyond its borders. The pace and scope of China's military build-up already puts regional military balances at risk[29].

China's conventional strike capability is centered around the Sukhoi and J-11 role aircraft fleet. The capability of Sukhoi fleet is augmented by two other major fighter production programs; the indigenous J-10 and JH-7A program. The J-10 program, which has been under way for over two decades, has made considerable progress especially after the late 1990s. While some small initial batches have been delivered, recent orders for Russian AI-31 turbofan engines may indicate China is ready to begin major production infusion of technology from Israel (as used in the Lavi fighter programme, a model that itself borrowed heavily from the US made F-16).[30] Thus, it has an adequately large combat aircraft fleet to give strategic teeth to its force projection options. However, the problem area for China is the paucity of 'Combat enablers' i.e., fleet of airlift, tankers and C2ISR platforms which create a "force multiplier effect" and provide extended reach for power projection.

The core of China's Strategic capable airlift fleet is the twenty IL-76 transporters procured from Russia in the 1990s. Similar in capability to the US C-141B, the IL-76 provides a significant payload and range combination which can be used to support air land cargo

[29] US office of Secretary of Defence Quadrennial Defense Review Report 2006, www://http://www.defenselink.mil/qdr/report/Report 20060203.pdf.29

[30] Richard D Fisher, Jr, "Impact of Foreign Weapon Systems and Technology on the Modernisation of the Peoples Liberation Army," (Air Force Systems: Foreign Assistance for the Chengalu J-10), Report for the US China Economic and Security Review Commission.

operations across China—or beyond. China and Russia have also announced that PLAAF would procure an additional 30 IL-76 transports.[31] This development represents a major increase in the strategic airlift capability of PLAAF. And in the event of a major conflict, China can also be expected to rely upon a large fleet of commercial airliners currently in use by state controlled airlines. These aircrafts may not be able to perform unique military missions such as air-drop and air-land operations into un-improved and under-developed airfields but will significantly enhance. PLAAF's palletized capability to move expeditionary forces and palletized freight over long distances thereby helping China's cause in projecting conventional force beyond China's periphery.

The air-borne capability of China resides with PLAAF. The 15th Airborne Army represents the PLA's primary rapid reaction capability and provides a unique capability for China's armed forces to reach out to seize an objective and either hold it till additional conventional forces can be brought in or withdraw once the immediate objective is achieved. The fact that airborne forces are considered to be one of the most trained in the PLA adds to the importance of their role in any rapid projection of conventional force by China. This 15th Airborne Army is composed of three divisions, the 43rd, 44th and 45th; each with roughly 10,000 soldiers. These forces play a key role in how China would fight in Taiwan, and could be expected to do the same in other scenarios in which their unique capabilities in force projection can be advantageously utilized. However, the primary handicap of this Airborne Army remains lack of strategic mobility which will get considerably enhanced once all the 30 contracted IL-76, are supplied by Russia. With a total fleet of 50 large aircrafts, the PLAAF will not feel compelled to immediately look for China's civil aviation fleet not only for undertaking force projection operations but also during humanitarian relief operations as part of force projection intent.

---

[31] "China to Buy Russian Jetsfor $1.5Bln" Associated Press, Sept 9, 2008.

Any discussion on power projection would be incomplete without taking into account the refueling capability of the air-assets. China, as of now, seems to be constrained by this limitation. Its force projection options are limited to the combat radius of its existing fleet with presumption that the PLAAF airfield at Lhasa is affected by winter weather and are unavailable for operations for the majority of the year. Once the complete fleet of eight IL-78s is received (perhaps by 2020) it will be able to support the compatible strike aircrafts such as Su-30. With tanker support, the range of strike aircraft is theoretically unlimited although in practice the limitation continues in terms of aircrew fatigue. In a coercive application of expeditionary force, PLAAF, using IL-78 tankers, will be able to achieve an extended radius of 2600 kms with one refueling and 3500 kms after a second refueling. Thus, the increased range brought about by the tanker support brings the Malacca Strait within the 2600 km ring while the Strait of Hormuz would still remain slightly outside the 3500 km (unless Lhasa is available).

Another significant step in terms of China's ability to rapidly employ conventional force on a global scale is the use of facilities on foreign soil to extend the range of PLAAF assets. Chinese activities in the Indian Ocean Region such as establishment of a listening post on Great Coco Island, construction of a base on Small Coco Island in Bay of Bengal, construction of port facilities at Gwadar in Pakistan, building of a 12,400 foot long runway in Myanmar and assistance to Sri Lanka in the construction of a modern commercial port at Hambantota on the southern tip of the island nation suggest that China may have intentions to exploit these facilities in the eventuality of undertaking force projection operations to assert itself as a regional power. Whether there are agreements in place with host nations to permit the PLA to operate from these facilities in a contingency remains to be seen.

Thus, the PLA today possesses a rough but ready force projection capability, one that will continue to steadily improve over time, which adds greater risks and costs for potential opponents in China's periphery. The modernizing PLA increasingly provides the Chinese leadership with credible coercive strength—one that can back up the threat of force and for selective employment of force to promote China's national sovereignty and security interests along its land, air and maritime borders[32].

PAKISTAN

Pakistan, since its independence, has apparently been dominated by the fear of an existential threat from its enormous neighbour on the East i.e. India. This perhaps justifies the reason for successive Pakistan Governments, be it civil or military, to view their national security interests through a distorted India-centric strategic lens. This emphasis on military security has contributed to the overwhelming influence of the armed forces, above all the army, in policy and governance through most of Pakistan's history.[33] Quite surprisingly, Pakistan has largely been successful in making the international community believe that its survival as a nation state has always been threatened because of which it has to focus its grand strategy around certain principal issues namely:

- Maintain sufficient conventional strength to deter an Indian attack.

- In case deterrence fails, it should be able to prevent a catastrophic defeat so as to allow international community to intervene either diplomatically or militarily to restore adverse situation.

- Have adequate nuclear deterrence capability.

---

[32] Susan M Puska, "Rough But Ready Force Projection: An Assessment of Recent PLA Training".

[33] Ayesha Siddiqa Agha, "Pakistan's Security: Problems of Linearity," South Asian Journal No.3 (January-March 2004)

- Conflate and coalesce diplomatic assistance, moral support and weapons/ technology transfer from world community.

- Translate its geo-strategic position into an advantageous bargaining platform as has been done in the case of Afghanistan crisis and support it (Pakistan) has offered to the US and the coalition forces.

- Remain vitally concerned about developments in its immediate neighbourhood comprising India, Iran, Afghanistan and Central Asian Republics (CAR).

- Pursue low cost means of destabilizing India through covert/ overt support to the *"jihadis".*

While this fundamental strategic paradigm rightfully serves Pakistan's immediate interests, it may not succeed in bolstering it's geo-strategic stature and potential to be a dominant and key player in the regional security calculus since it forces Pakistan to worry more about its mere existence than on donning the mantle of a key regional player. This traditional self-perceived 'successful' strategy may provide an immediate successor to the policy makers and rulers in Pakistan but whether it will further Pakistan's cause as a strategic player in 21st century is a debatable preposition since there have been no indications or signs to suggest Pakistan's desire to assert itself through force projection operations. Today Pakistan Army suffers from a number of critical deficiencies that retard its progress towards becoming a regional power that can project itself to safeguard its geo-strategic, military or socio-economic interests. Some of the parameters that need to be analysed in this regard are:-

- Small Pakistan Navy sans any Carrier Battle Group (CBG) may be able to look after the nation's defence concerns but may be grossly inadequate to support any force projection designs.

- • Limited mobility in terms of Pak's strategic airlift capability aggravates Pakistan's force projection dilemma.

- • Large, professional and well-trained army may be competent to thwart any external aggression on its mainland but lacks any experience at force projection operations.

- • Ability to undertake joint operations is another grey area for Pakistan. Despite presence of a joint staff at the national level and discussions of inter-service cooperation, the three services have traditionally trained and fought in near isolation from each other which is detrimental to the successful conduct of any force projection operation.

- • Army's command structure is also problematic since all nine Corps' are controlled directly from General Headquarters (GHQ).[34]

- • Continued pre-occupation with fundamentalist activities diverts its efforts towards assisting non-state actors and weans its attention away from legitimate regional dominance through internationally acceptable operations.

- • Deficiencies in technology, mobility, logistics, doctrine and military culture have compromised Pakistan's geo-strategic ability to translate its military capabilities into a comprehensive force projection dimension.

Notwithstanding the above limitations, it would be naïve for any country in the world today to take its eyes off the 'international canvas' that is susceptible to discoloration with every single incident that has international ramifications – be it 9/11 in US, 13/12 in New Delhi or 26/11 in Mumbai. Pakistan therefore is no exception. It's obsession with fundamentalism and self prophesized prognostication as messiah of 'Islamic World' may force it to undertake limited force

---

[34] Jane's Sentinel Security Assessment – South Asia; Pakistan; June 13, 2005

projection operations with whatever meagre resources at its disposal in those regions and countries where it has ethno-religious and geo-strategic stakes. Such force projection endeavors, even at margins, might suffice to stave off any designs by the aggressor or subvert or to toggle Pakistan's position as an emerging power amongst the Islamic World. Thus, the possibility of Pakistan undertaking limited force projection operations on its periphery and in the IOR cannot be totally discounted. Coupled with this, Pakistan's contribution towards peace keeping missions, humanitarian aid, and assistance during calamities and towards restoration of adverse situation in small island states will surely qualify for appellation as force projection operation.

NATO

The essential purpose of NATO with its 26 member states is to *safeguard the freedom and security of all its members by political and military means.*[35] To meet the ongoing challenges and threats that are staring and ogling at the world community today NATO decided at the Prague Summit in November 2002 to adapt its operational capabilities which included creation of an effective and technologically advanced response force, designed to be flexible, rapidly deployable, interoperable and sustainable. This force is meant to function on three different concepts as discussed hereunder in succeeding paragraphs.

NATO REACTIONERY FORCE (NRF) CONCEPT

NRF would draw forces from a rotational pool of land, maritime and air forces fully supported by NATO's collective assets like AWACS and NATO's command structure. The force operates within the full spectrum of missions world over and functions under the Joint Task Force Headquarters. It is supposed to be having a 'forced entry capability' and can operate as a 'stand alone force' as well. The organisation works on a modular concept which makes it possible

---

[35] NATO Office of Information and Press. NATO Handbook(Brussels: NATO,2001), 30

to initiate an operation with only certain selected elements of the NRF. When fully deployed the size of NRF can go beyond 20,000 personnel. The "Initial Operational Capability of NRF"[36] could be:

- **Command Element**: A three-star HQ, forward deployed by one of NATO's Joint Forces Command HQ.

- **Major Units: Land Component**

  - 3 x Infantry Battalions (airborne, and/or airmobile and**/or** Mechanized Battalions)

  - Artillery Battalion

  - Engineer Company

  - Air Defense Company

  - Electronic Warfare Company

  - CBRN Battalion (Chemical, Biological, Radiological and Nuclear battalion)

  - Logistic Battalion

  - 2 x Helicopter Squadrons

- **Major Units: Air Component**

  - 7 x Fighter Squadrons

  - Air-to-Air refuelling Squadron

  - SAM and Stinger Company

  - EW Squadron and UAV Platoon

  - Air Base Support Unit, including an Engineer Company

---

[36] "Trans-Atlantic Force Projection, What is the Best Solution:US,NATO, EU, or a Coalition", http://oai.dtic.mil/oai

- **Major Units: Maritime Component**

  - Aircraft Carrier

  - 10 x Frigates

  - 2 x Submarines

  - 4 x Maritime Patrol Aircrafts

  - 9 x Mine Countermine Ships

  - 1 x Amphibious Battalion

  - 2 x Landing Platform Docks

  - Squadron Attack Helicopters

  - Supply Ship

- **Major Units: SF Component**

  - CJSOTF HQ (Combined Joint Special Operations Task Force Headquarters)

  - 4 x SO Task Groups

Comments on NRF Concept

NRF is a multi-national unit. Any NRF Task Force would entail participation by 10 to 20 nations. Such a multi-national force may accord an international authenticity and legitimacy but shall pose immense coordination problems which would be further aggravated by the "interoperability paradigm". Moreover, the charter specifies that NRF can be deployed only once a consensus has been achieved amongst all the 26 member states, irrespective of the fact that they may or may not be contributing any contingent to the NRF being earmarked for deployment. Coupled with this is the caveat that the force would be deployed only after ratification of the need to deploy military force by the North Atlantic Council (NAC). Achieving consensus with such myriad national interests, amidst 'diverse' geo-political and socio-economic agendas, will itself pose daunting, discomfit, and confounding challenges for the NAC. Reliability and endurance in terms of periodicity of deployment of such a force would therefore be under scanner. However, an assuredly positive side of such a force rests in the fact that it is a complete 'combined arms force' with all the enablers that enhance its international credibility with reasonable degree of 'assured success'. Another significant development relates to the position of the US within the overall gambit of deployment of NRF. Although the US has a dominant position within NATO, a NATO deployment is not perceived as a US unilateral action or even as a US backed deployment. Therefore, when a NATO intervention will take place, especially within NATO's area of responsibility, then the acceptance quotient in the world will be reasonably high.

EU Battlegroups

Since its inception, European Union has remained fully committed towards global peace, prosperity and collective development of the entire region. Its charter allows it to focus its efforts on global security, political and regional stability, effective multilateralism, non-proliferation of Weapons of Mass Destruction (WMD), anti-terror campaigns, peace keeping missions, disaster management and crisis management operations. Some of the developments directly related to EU and meriting attention are:-

- The Maastricht Treaty of 1991 recommended the formation of a Common Foreign and Security Policy (CFSP) for the EU. The treaty also envisages framing of a common defence policy.

- In 2003, the Helsinki Headline Goal[37] proposed a RRF of 50,000 to 60,000 troops by 2003 itself. This RRF was to

---

[37] European Council. *Headline Goal 2003,* (Helsinki, 10-11 December 1999).

have the ability to deploy within 60 days with a sustainability of at least one year post deployment. However, this deadline of 2003 could not be achieved.

- In 2004, a new Headline Goal was developed which recommended formation of multiple, small and rapidly deployable Battle Groups, which were to be effective by 2007. The deadline was met by UK, France and Germany who adopted the Battle Group Concept.

These Battle Groups have the ability to 'deploy within 15 days with roughly 1500 personnel, including combat support and combat service support units'.[38] The composition of these Battle Groups is as follows:-

- Commanded by   :   Brigadier/Equivalent
- Major Units   :   One Infantry Battalion

                               One Engineer Squadron

                               One Light Artillery Battery

                               One Det Air Defence Battery

                               One Support Squadron

Comments on EU Battle Groups

In the case of EU Battle Groups also, there will be a need to have a consensus among the sovereign member states before mobilizing and inducting these groups into a combat zone. Situation will be even more complicated in the backdrop of the fact that 'there are several non-aligned and neutral EU members like Ireland, Sweden, Finland and Austria that play an important role. These nations do not improve the military effectiveness of the EU'. On the contrary, they can significantly delay the entire decision process with regard to deployment of the Battle Groups.

---

[38] European Council. *EU Battlegroups Concept* (Brussels, 6 May 2004).

Within EU, the process of "giving away or compromising sovereignty" is already happening in economic and monetary policy issues but policies and matters related to military will always have security implications that will govern the internal politico-diplomatic affairs of each nation state. Looking at the military power of the EU, there is enough scope to enhance the existing military capabilities since the existing battle groups are small in composition, both equipment-wise as well as manpower-wise. Moreover, these groups are not fully synergistic due to absence of an effective and widely acceptable C2 structure. Thus, from an economic and diplomatic perspective the EU may be a giant, but from a military perspective it is yet to play any major contributory role.

A Tailor Made Coalition Force

Deployment of a tailor made coalition force under the NATO flag is considered as the best option since it does not necessarily entail reaching any consensus among all the member states. Military intervention, preferably with a broad base, provides a good alternative to the consensus option needed for the NRF or EU Battle Groups. In this case the forces of the involved countries will lay adequate emphasis on selection of the task force to ensure a very high degree of success rate for the projection force. The effectiveness of such a coalition force largely depends upon the core capabilities of certain select nations who have a technological edge in terms of the overall capabilities of their defence forces. The impact of information, intelligence, finance and economic sustainability of such a force are given due deliberation by the commanders and planners. Coupled with this is the aspect of public opinion and acceptance among the donor nations who need to support the launch of such a coalition force.

Force Projection by NATO in Afghanistan

It may be apt to analyze the NATO's role in the ongoing Afghanistan crisis which incidentally, is the first coordinated and synergistic endeavour by NATO in projecting its collective strength. The decision to deploy a multinational coalition force in Afghanistan was taken at the Bonn Conference in December 2001. The conference put its stamp on the decision to establish partnership between the United Nations, the Afghan Transitional Authority and the International Security Assistance Force (ISAF). The first ISAF was given the responsibility of maintaining security around Kabul. This force was led by the United Kingdom from Dec 2001 to June 2002 with contributions from 18 countries including 14 NATO members. The second 'six month rotation' was led by Turkey till February 2003 while the third one was constituted under Germany and the Netherlands from February 2003 to August 2003. Since then the NATO's contribution in Afghanistan has successfully continued with a three part structure that has been functioning smoothly. This three part structure is:-

- ISAF Headquarters [falls under the responsibility of Joint Forces Command North (JFC North) in Brunssum, the Netherlands].

- Air Port Task Force

- Kabul Multi-National Brigade.

This ISAF quickly forged ties with the US led Operation Enduring Freedom and the US Central Command (CENTCOM) and successfully coordinated logistics and flights in and out of the regions. While doing so they maintained their own identities and stuck to their own stated missions and objectives which included the following:-

- Provide basic security

- Enable NGOs to perform their work

- Assist Afghan government in regaining hold on the country

- Constitute Provincial Reconstruction Teams (PRTs) for providing surge and boost to the development work.

Thus far, the NATO's contribution towards sustaining expeditionary forces has been quite noteworthy which has established the credibility of NATO's potential as a dominant power. It has overcome the stigma of being a partisan outfit during the cold war when there was a "joke" going around regarding the purpose of NATO which said, "The purpose of NATO was to keep the Americans in, the Russians out and the Germans down." The Afghan experiment has indeed proved a success for NATO; though may not be in the outcome of the operation but definitely in the performance and credibility of this outfit.

Likely Future Scenario for NATO.

Future operations by NATO are likely to be undertaken in sync with the UN aspirations. Synergistic application of force in concert with US, EU and certain emerging global and regional power players like BRIC countries would be the hallmark of future operations by NATO. These operations may see new dimensions and concepts that would combine civil and military forces as well as certain Non-Governmental Organizations (NGOs) - all of which would strive to work in unison and harmony.

Certain issues that may emerge on the NATO's canvas are Arab-Israeli dispute, creation of mutually acceptable international borders between Palestine and Israel, consolidation in Afghanistan and possible intervention or assistance to Pakistan in flushing fundamentalists from inaccessible areas. NATO is also prepared to get involved in other stabilization and reconstruction work. Regardless of the region or the circumstances, the duration of any such operations will be measured in years, not months. Stabilization and reconstruction missions are aimed at tasks that are by definition long-term and somewhat open-ended as they gradually transition from more military tasks to more police-oriented and civil affairs tasks.[39] Therefore, like Bosnia, where NATO maintained a substantial presence for over a decade, the ongoing commitment in Afghanistan may also be a long term 'covenant'.

Lessons for India

The lesson for India - an aspirant regional power, would therefore be, to formulate suitable doctrines and policies that would facilitate prolonged commitment during force projection operations. It must also ensure close cooperation with other international actors, who may be equally prompt in responding to all such crises. Appropriate regulations will also have to be formulated by the government to ensure a common or shared funding by MEA, MHA, MoD and other Ministries for all such operations to avoid any delays either during their launch or subsequently during their prolonged commitment.

UNIITED STATES

Before dwelling on the current US policies and doctrines on the concept of force projection it may be appropriate to peep into the past and have a look at the US global interests a few decades ago. In the last quarter of the twentieth century, US had maintained strategic interests in the Persian Gulf. It demonstrated its willingness to use military force in the area as a diplomatic signal, if not as an expeditionary design. Subsequently, the Yom Kippur War of 1973, prolonged the US – Soviet confrontation on numerous issues and the oil embargo of 1974 led to an American warning that "American military intervention to protect vital oil supplies" was a possibility. By late 1970's the US had begun to contemplate the use of military force to ensure an uninterrupted flow of oil for itself. Therefore, in 1977 President Carter signed a Presidential Directive in which one of the proposals was to have a Rapid Deployment force. Accordingly, two Army Divisions (82nd and 101st) and one Marine Division were earmarked for such duties. However, it was the year 1979 when US realized that its strategic interests and geo-political dominance was

[39] 168 DSC 05-E NATO Out of Area Operations, 2005 Annual session

being challenged as would be evident from the following developments of that era:-

- Failure to ratify SALT II Treaty whose debate "revealed to both the Congress and the American Public, the degree to which the US military power had been permitted to deteriorate in the face of an unstinting and comprehensive Soviet build up.

- Overthrow of the Shah in Iran by anti-western Islamic fundamentalists.

- Third and perhaps the most important development was the Soviet invasion of Afghanistan in Dec 1979.

All these developments led to a reappraisal of US policy which led to the formulation of "Carter Doctrine" that stated, "any attempt by a foreign power to gain control of the Persian Gulf and surrounding area would be regarded as an attack on the vital interests of the USA, and be stopped by all means necessary including the use of military force."[40] This was the first formal commitment of the US military power towards force projection in the region.

Consequent to these developments a Rapid Deployment Joint Task Force (RDJTF) was activated in March 1980. It was placed under the US Readiness Command. The aim of this force was, "Deterrence against possible Soviet or proxy invasion, conflict among the states of the area and subversion and insurrection within the states and thus help maintain regional stability and the Gulf-oil flow westward".[41] The RDJTF was designed to be flexible with forces being drawn, during crisis, from a central pool of resources. The composition of this task force was as follows:-

---

[40] The Carter Doctrine and the creation of a New Force, http://www.historyofwar.org/articles/weapons_rdf.html

[41] The Rapid Deployment Task force, http://www.historyofwar.org/articles

- Headquarters staff was drawn from all the services

- Commander of the JTF was a three star officer who used to be appointed rotationally by Army and Navy

- Deputy Commander was an Air Force Officer

- At two star levels there were component commanders and their staffs

- Each defence service earmarked substantial assets as discussed below:

  - **Army:** Following resources were assigned by the Army:-

    - 82nd Airborne Division – (consisted of eight infantry battalions in three brigades with a total strength of 16000 troops and substantial organic airlift in terms of helicopter assets).

    - 101st Air Assault Division – (with massed assault helicopter capability and three brigades with three battalions each having a total strength of approx 18000 personnel).

    - 6th Cavalry Brigade – (Comprising two Aviation Squadrons with support, communication and HQ elements).

    - 24th Mechanised Division.

    - 9th Infantry Division – (Was conceived as a 'High Technology Light Division' with emphasis on 'heavy firepower, long range mobility, Light Forces with long range weapons and improved C3 and real-time information systems to achieve extended battlefield concept'.

- Marine Corps: The Marine contribution was as follows:-

  1st Marine Division

  3rd Marine Air Wing

  1st Force Service Support Group

  7th Amphibious Brigade

- **Navy:** Following resources were provided by the US Navy:-

  - Three Carrier Battle Groups (one each in the Indian Ocean, Mediterranean Sea and the Pacific Ocean).

  - One Surface Action Group.

  - Anti-Submarine Warfare Patrol Aircraft.

  - Amphibious Ships.

- **Air Force:** Air Force committed the under mentioned assets:-

  - 07 Tactical Fighter Wings (TFWs)

  - 03 Tactical Fighter Groups (TFGs)

  - 01 Tactical Reconnaissance Group (TRGs)

  - 01 EW Group

  - 01 AEW & C Wing

  - Civil Reserve Air Fleet (CRAF) with long range cargo and long range passenger aircrafts was placed 'on call'.

Thus, a truly joint force having a balanced composition in terms of resources, as well as the command and control structure, had descended on the horizon to announce the US's resolve to project itself as a power that had a 'global reach' in pursuit of defending its strategic interests through forward presence. The consolidation of this concept and struggle for dominance continued through the next couple of decades till the disintegration of erstwhile USSR transformed the bipolar world into a unipolar entity in 1991.

This end of Cold War and the tragic events of 9/11 serve as two landmark events that perhaps forced United States to have a fresh look at the National Security Strategy. It had to transform its strategic outlook of containment, deterrence and confrontation with communism to an asymmetric and unconventional war against spread of fundamentalist tendencies. It had to switch from the erstwhile concept of large scale deployment of conventional forces primarily structured to fight the Soviet Union on the basis of "forward deployment" and "overseas military bases" to the concept of "power projection" or "force projection" which essentially denotes the ability of a nation to apply all the necessary elements of national power, at the place and time necessary, to achieve national security objectives. These elements include political, diplomatic, economic and military power of a nation.

The US believes that an effective and demonstrated power projection capability can promote security and deter the aggression of potential adversaries, demonstrate resolve, and if necessary, enable successful military operations anywhere in the world. It soon realized that the geo-strategic and geo-political dynamics have changed in a manner that the security threats now encompass a three tiered range of conflict scenarios. The first level consists of "Core security challenges" that affect the vital national interests of the United States. These challenges include catastrophic terrorism, an increasingly powerful and assertive China and possibly re-emergence of Russian Power. The second level involves potential conflicts in the Persian Gulf and / or the Korean peninsula. The third level includes, but is not limited to Peace Keeping and Humanitarian Operations, which comprise those lesser contingencies that US forces may have to support from time to time. The most important aspects of these multiple threats is that they no longer present a situation where US military forces would fight a single opponent in a conventional manner at the known location and time. It will function along a 'spectrum of conflict' transiting between lower and higher levels without losing momentum.[42] This full spectrum of conflict, in essence, implies that the strategic, operational and tactical deployment of forces should be understood as one seamless process and not as three distinctly separate phases.

Today, Force Projection is an integral part of the US military strategy and aims at promoting security and deterring aggression by honing its ability to mobilize and deploy rapidly in any and every corner of the globe to deal with and neutralize any threat that US or its citizens may face. In fact, the former US President George W Bush, while speaking on National Security Strategy to West Point Cadets in 2002 stated, "If we wait for threats to fully materialize, we will have waited too long. In the world we have entered, the only path to safety is the path of action. And this nation will act."[43] The new, pre-emptive National Security Strategy, referred to by many as the "Bush Doctrine" will have a significant impact on the military role in power projection. The National Security Strategy (NSS) published in September 2002 states that the primary security objective is to protect the United States and its allies from rogue states and their terrorist clients before they are able to threaten or use weapons of mass destruction. The strategy further outlines the objectives, operational

---

[42] Power Projection and the National Security Strategy; http://www.allacademic.com/meta/pmlopa research citation

[43] USAWC Strategy Research Project; http://www.fas.org/man/eprint/zeigles.pdf

concepts and resources required for successful implementation of the NMS. These NMS objectives include:-

- Defending the US Homeland

- Promote security

- Deter aggression

- Win the Nation's War, and

- Ensure Military Superiority

To achieve these objectives, the strategy calls for the execution of multiple, simultaneous and synchronized military operational concepts. These concepts are designed to protect the US homeland and interests abroad, prevent conflict and unwarned attacks and prevail against adversaries in a wide range of possible contingencies.[44] While doing so, the US is believed to be exploiting the full potential of its allies in terms of military power and infrastructural back up. It is also open to establishment of new alliances and partnerships for furtherance of its objective.

US Joint Forces Command (USJFCOM) is a strong proponent of Joint Force Projection Concept which it has described as a "responsive and adaptive knowledge-based process that enables decision makers at all levels the ability to make timely, accurate decisions and risk assessments for global force projection." JPF doctrine provides the joint force with an integrated set of capabilities to conduct net-centric, end-to-end joint deployment, planning, analysis and execution activities during joint force projection operations. However, it (US) continues to believe that the option of "prevention" will retain a dominant position in the strategic precepts and will necessitate pre-positioning of suitable forces in pre-determined areas throughout the world. Such pre-positioned forces

---

[44] Col Jack C Zeigler Jr and Col Charlee W Higbee, The Army Special Operation Forces Role in Force Projection, www.fas.org/man/eprint

will have comprehensive capabilities in terms of operational teeth and administrative tail suitably complemented by the host country that agrees to allow such pre-positioning. The Joint Strategic Capabilities Plan (JSCP) is therefore prepared to consider all such options that are available to such pre-positioned forces for meeting their specified objective. Once these "forwardly-present" forces are considered to be inadequate, either collectively or partially, then a decision is taken to project additional contingents either from the Continental United States (CONUS) or from another closeby forward base. The option of arriving at an agreement with an ally who is in the vicinity of the target area is also explored. The concept supplements and demonstrates US's resolve of projecting and employing military power 'from dispersed locations to overwhelm any adversary and control any situation, while maintaining the flexibility to rapidly conduct and sustain multiple, simultaneous missions in geographically separated and environmentally diverse regions of the world'.[45] The US FM 100-7 defines "power projection as the ability of the US to apply any combination of economic, diplomatic, informational or military instruments of national power".[46] Till the end of Cold War the US, therefore, had adopted the doctrine of placing reliance on force projection by way of rapid deployment of combat power to any region in the world and sustain them for missions spanning the operational continuum. Within that framework, the defence forces contribution to force projection is the demonstrated ability to rapidly alert, mobilize and field a force that is deployable, lethal, versatile, expandable and sustainable.[47]

Lastly, and most importantly, the US concept of utilizing the US Army Reserve (USAR) for force projection operations merits attention and emulation. It has a concept of seamless integration of its regular forces with the reserve forces. Its Army reserves have proven itself

---

[45] PP3, ibid

[46] FM::100-10-1

[47] FM: 110-10-1, Chapter 1, Power Projection.

to be an essential partner in America's Army. In recent years, the Army Reserve has participated in a wide variety of contingencies including Operation Desert Shield and Operation Desert Storm where 35 percent of all Army forces were from the Army Reserve and the intervention in Haiti, where over 70 percent of all reserve component forces mobilized were Army Reserve personnel. Today 47 percent of the Army's combat service support assets are found within the Army Reserve.[48] Thus, the Reserve components have immense ability to supplement a nation's comprehensive force projection capability and reduce substantially, the challenges in terms of resource constraints in all such force projection operations.

---

[48] Maj Hilda Martinez and Maj Lisa Tepas, Army Reserve Role in Force Projection, p2

CHAPTER 6

INDIAN EXPERIENCE IN FORCE PROJECTION

*The world is a dangerous place, not because of those who do evil,
but because of those who look on and do nothing.*

- Albert Einstein

Indian armed forces have participated in numerous peace keeping missions under the aegis of United Nations for over 50 years now. Although these missions cannot be termed as the force projection forays, they definitely lend credibility to India's rightful claims as an emerging power, not necessarily at a global level but surely in the regional parlance. Such missions have not only helped our defence forces but also the political and diplomatic policy makers in understanding the global security dynamics and have provided them an insight into the entire gamut of force projection and multitude of activities that would contribute handsomely towards cementing our claim as a regional power. Ever since our first commitment on UN assignment after the Korean War, our learning curve and participation has consistently seen an upward surge with apt recognition from the global community. Some of our noticeable footprints over the years have been:

§   **Korea**

- India contributed a Para Field Ambulance unit to the UN force under General Douglas MacArthur. The unit

MIDDLE EAST : GAZA

participated in airborne mission alongwith American troops. It treated almost 2,000 battle casualties and close to 10,000 sick and injured in Korea.

- Indian Custodian force under Major General SPP Thorat took custody of over 20,000 prisoners of war till their final disposal.

- This Indian Custodian Force handled the situation with compassion, patience, neutrality and humaneness which earned it accolades and admirations world over.

§ **United Nations Emerging Force (UNEF-1), Gaza**

- In Dec 1956, an Infantry Battalion Group was sent to Gaza, as shown in the map, to monitor the buffer zone between Egypt and the Anglo-French Forces.

- The tasks of Indian contingents were:-

  - Monitor withdrawal of Israeli forces from Sinai Peninsula.

  - Supervise cessation of hostilities between Egypt and Israel along the Armistice Demarcation Line (ADL).

  - Ensure smooth exchange of prisoners of war.

- Indian commitment continued till May 1967 when war broke out between Egypt and Israel.

- Thus, for more than 11 years, the Indian contingent effectively maintained peace in one of the most sensitive areas of the Middle East, thereby sowing the seeds of Indian intentions of "projecting itself overseas" — albeit through peace keeping missions.

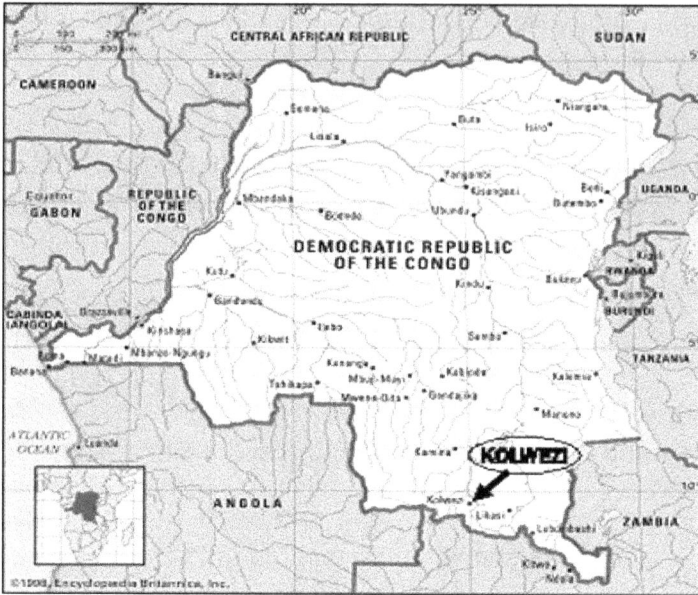

CONGO

§ **Congo**

- In 1961 India contributed one Infantry Brigade Group for conduct of military operations in Congo.

- This was the first time when India successfully conducted its first peace enforcement operations under the aegis of United Nations.

- Indian Brigade took the rebels by complete surprise and secured the town of Kowlezi, as depicted in the map. This paved the way for reunification of Congo.

§ **Cambodia (UNTAC)**

- Indian contingent for UNTAC comprised following elements:-

  o One Infantry Battalion Group

  o Mine Training Team

  o Field Ambulance Company

  o Staff to UNTAC HQs

  o Military Observers

  o The tasks assigned to them were:

    - Disarm

    - Provide secure environment for the voters

    - Ensure electoral security

    - Large scale demining operations in conjunction with teams from 14 nations

    - Provide medical cover to UN units/locals

SOMALIA

GULF OF ADEN

DJIBOUTI

AWDAL

SANAAG

BARI

WOQOOYI GALBEED

TOGDHEER

SOOL

NUGAAL

ETHIOPIA

Disputed Area

MUDUG

GALGUDUUD

BAKOOL HIRAAN

INDIAN OCEAN

GEDO

BAY

SHABEELLAHA DHEXE

MOGADISHU

JUBBADA DHEXE

KENYA

JUBBADA HOOSE

0   50 100 150 Kilometers

Copyright © 2007 Compare Infobase Limited

- The areas of operational responsibility included the three most politically sensitive provinces in Cambodia including underdeveloped and reasonably large province of Kampong Cham shown in the map.

- The Indian troops successfully demonstrated that the country has risen from the dour and obdurate parlors of the so called 'introverted democracy' to a nation that was willingly forthcoming to announce its willingness to play a role in regional geo-politics.

§ **Somalia (UNOSOM II)**

- Somalia commitment saw participation of Indian Navy for the first time and set the foundations for larger naval role in projecting India's intentions and capabilities away from homeland. The force composition for the Somalia included following:-

  o All arms Infantry Brigade Group

  o Armoured component

  o Helicopters

  o Warships of Indian Navy

  o Logistics units/sub units

- Indian Brigade won accolades from the international community for deft handling of humanitarian assistance and civic action programs under extremely challenging conditions.

- UNOSOM II also afforded a unique opportunity to Indian Defence Forces to demonstrate a very high level of tri-service integration and coordination in undertaking a conglomerate mix of counter-guerilla operations, provision of humanitarian assistance and carrying out rehabilitation and restoration work with utmost synergy and cohesiveness.

§   **Other Assignments:** Besides these seminally historical, precedent setting and pivotal contributions, India has been a part of numerous other peace-keeping operations that have reinforced its capabilities as a 'regional player' having enough potential to influence the outcome of crisis like situations faced by the global community.

It would be appropriate to concede that calling any of the above mentioned contributions as "force projection" would be naive, perhaps foolishly credulous and gullible; but it would be equally unpretentious not to acknowledge that these contributions did set the stage for India to supplicate and stake its rightful claim for recognition as an emerging power. In some manner, successful accomplishments of these commitments must have emboldened Indian Policy makers to take a plunge in solving the Sri Lankan and Maldivian crisis which come quite close to being qualified as 'force projection' operations by India although critics may argue that these operations may best be termed as mere 'peace keeping' missions. In this regard, Mr Kuldeep Sahadev, IFS (Retd), Former Ambassador, who was Joint Secretary in charge of Sri Lanka during the negotiations and signing of the Sri Lanka Agreement in 1987 and during IPKF operations had this to say:-

> *"The Indo-Sri Lankan Agreement and the dispatch of the IPKF were not really conceived by us as Force Projection. Our attempt was to resolve a problem which was creating instability in our neighbourhood and was beginning to create political problems for us domestically. But there is no denying that operationally it became an exercise in Force Projection and I am sure it was an exercise from which the Indian Armed Forces would have learnt many lessons and gained valuable experience."*[49]

---

[49] Proceedings on Seminar on Indian Experience in Force Projection conducted by CENJOWS, 15-16 Sep 2008, pp 21.

In fact Sri Lanka and Maldives are the only two instances of our 'force projection' intent in which there was some semblance of a synergistic application of integrated national power. The uniqueness of these two operations lay in the fact that they were bilateral and not under UN mandate.

Force Projection in Sri Lanka

Sri Lankan commitment was perhaps the first instance when Indian troops went abroad in a bilateral arrangement at the invitation of the government of the host country. The Indo-Sri Lanka Agreement of 29 July 1987 provided the legal framework for inducting an Indian Peace Keeping Force (IPKF) into Sri Lanka with India agreeing to "underwrite and guarantee the resolutions and cooperate in the implementation of these proposals" [Article 2.14 of Agreement]. India, in consonance with Sri Lankan demand, further undertook to provide military assistance for implementing the proposals on "as and when required basis." [Refer Article 2.16 (c)]. This obligation was amplified in an Annexure to the Agreement which specifically visualized that "an Indian peace-keeping contingent may be invited by the President of Sri Lanka to guarantee and enforce the cessation of hostilities, if so required." A rigid time-frame to end the ethnic conflict was also envisaged [Article 2.9]. The worked out time frame was:-

- Cessation of hostilities within 48 hours of the Agreement being signed.

- All arms held by the militant groups to be surrendered to authorities designated by Sri Lankan government [the Annexure recommended the presence of representatives of the Sri Lankan and Indian Red Cross].

- Following the cessation of hostilities and surrender of arms the [Sri Lankan] army and security personnel would be confined to barracks.

- The process of surrendering arms and confining of security personnel to barracks would be completed within 72 hours of cessation of hostilities.

- The emergency would be lifted in the Eastern and Northern provinces by 15 August 1987.

Consequent to signing of this Agreement, the deployment of the Indian Defence Forces commenced on 30 July 1987, just the very next day of signing of the Agreement. However, prior to this deployment Indian Air Force had launched a "humanitarian operation" code named "Operation Eagle" in which food supplies were air-dropped over the Jaffna Peninsula on 04 June 1987. Significant point to note was that the operation was not undertaken by transport aircrafts alone; instead they were escorted by Mirage-2000 multi-role war planes; thus conveying to Sri Lanka, in particular, and the world in general, that India was ready to intervene militarily should its geo-political and strategic interests demand so. The message was loud and clear, and vociferous enough, to be perceived by the world community that India was not to be trifled with since it had the will and the will power to address its national and regional security issues and would not allow anyone to 'flex muscle' in its neighbourhood. The so called 'docile and sleeping giant' had thus announced its arrival in the global "power dynamics console" to take control of its regional aspirations.

Background to IPKF Deployment

The background under which the force projection by IPKF was undertaken rested on the trilogy of our domestic, foreign and defence policies. As far as the domestic policy was concerned it was due to our affinity with the Tamilians who influenced the government to take the same action as was done in 1971 for the creation of Bangladesh and express solidarity with the ethnic minorities in Sri Lanka. The defence policy compulsions were the Sri Lanka's strategic location and importance of the Trincomalee harbour through which most of the maritime communication lanes pass. As far as the foreign policy is concerned, we had the compulsions of ensuring good relations and a supportive role in the moment of crisis because of our friendly ties; and also since Sri Lanka happened to be a member of the SAARC community. With these compulsions, India resorted to a coercive diplomacy to address the Sri Lankan problem. A sea armada was dispatched which was returned by Sri Lanka. This was followed by air drops duly supported by fighter planes which flew over the Sri Lankan skies and conveyed the message regarding India's inescapable interests and unavoidable involvement in the crisis.

The clearest geo-political explanation for sending the IPKF to Sri Lanka was provided by Shri J N Dixit, Former High Commissioner to Sri Lanka in an 'address to a largely military audience'[50] and deserves special notice. The reasons for the IPKF induction according to him were:-

- To preserve our own unity; to ensure the success of a very difficult experiment [creating an integrated nation out of a multi-lingual, multi-religious and multi-ethnic society];

- To counter the Sri Lankan government that started looking for external support to counter Tamil militancy, which had security implications for us; [these security implications included raising the strength of the Sri Lankan army and Para military forces, increased naval visits by the US and British navies, inviting foreign mercenaries and intelligence agencies to assist its operations, seeking assistance from Pakistan to train its Home Guards and Navy, offering broadcasting facilities to VOA, and buying arms from other countries inimical to India].

- To respect the sentiments of Tamil citizens of India.

---

[50] Pran Chopra, "Security, Sovereignty and India-Sri Lanka Relations", pp 110.

In Dixit's view, "Our strategic thinking has to take into account potential danger— [that] can be a creation of circumstances in neighbouring countries generating political and social trends in these countries which can have a ripple effect on our polity and disintegrate us." Quite surprisingly, there is a contrasting view aired by the then Sri Lankan President Jayewardene who cited outbreak of violence in the country as the pre-dominant reason that necessitated the induction of IPKF. He had this to say:

> "When Rajiv Gandhi visited Sri Lanka to sign the Agreement, I turned to the Chiefs of the Security Forces. They said they could spare some men [to control the situation] but did not have the planes to bring them from the north and east. Rajiv heard of my difficulty, and asked, "Can I help?" I told him of our difficulties and he said he will get some planes to transport our troops. Then he also asked whether I also needed some manpower to assist in the north and east. This was possible under the Accord. I said, "Since the planes are coming empty, why not send some?" That is how Indian troops came to Sri Lanka.[51]

It is evidently clear from the above inputs that lot more deliberations could have been done before launching the IPKF in haste, especially so, since India had not had any past experience in "force projection" operations and Sri Lanka chapter would serve as a 'precedence' for subsequent endeavours of this magnitude and intent.

Lessons of the IPKF Experience

Since our objective is not to study the IPKF operations in its entirety, we will remain focused on our aim of recommending 'force projection options for India.' Therefore, we would not discuss the details of operations conducted by IPKF, its mobilization and induction, its

---

[51] Sunday Times, 11 February 1990, during the course of an interview.

deployment pattern, execution of operations, logistic support and issues like deinduction. It would be appropriate for us to merely sniff and cull out certain lessons that may help us in future force projection assignments of similar nature. Some of these lessons have been elaborated in succeeding paragraphs:

- **Indicators of Success**

  - India's basic objective in sending its forces to Sri Lanka was "to preserve her democratic set up and territorial integrity seriously threatened by various militant groups and to ensure that the legitimate aspirations of its Tamil minorities were not neglected in the governance of that country. These objectives have been achieved in a large measure."[52]

  - Before induction, reasonably adequate ground conditions were created whereby political initiatives could be taken in the Tamil majority areas in Sri Lanka.

  - IPKF successfully ensured the safety of Sinhala and Tamil candidates in the Presidential and Parliamentary elections, enabling them to be conducted in conditions of near normalcy, and it is significant that the last round of general elections were held in Sri Lanka only eleven years earlier in 1977.[53]

  - IPKF succeeded in providing relief and rehabilitation to the displaced Tamils.

  - The force was successful in restoring the crippled essential services in the northern and eastern provinces "to help revive normal administration with electricity and

---

[52] Government of India, Ministry of Defence, Annual Report 1988-89, Supplement, p 5.

[53]   J N Dixit, "IPKF in Sri Lanka." P 256

water supply restored; and banks, courts, post and telegraph department, hospitals, educational institutions working. The conduct of '0' level examination was also arranged...........................".[54]

- IPKF had successfully eliminated the middle order leadership of LTTE and broken their stronghold over the Jaffna Peninsula.

- Elephant pass was open for the first time since LTTE had taken control of Jaffna.

- Sustained air operations in support of IPKF lasting 32 months entailed over 70,000 sorties by tactical transport aircrafts and helicopters. But it is not just the numbers. The helicopter missions, in particular, were flown over extremely difficult terrain and adverse weather conditions with cloud base at times lower than 100 feet.[55]

- A reasonably acceptable degree of jointmanship was achieved amongst the three services both, during the conduct of operations as well as for logistic back up.

- Credit must be given to the Indian Defence Forces, especially the Indian Navy and Indian Air Force for undertaking one of the largest shipments and airlifts since World War II. Not very many people would be aware that in terms of men and material, more tonnage was transported to Sri Lanka than in any theatre of operation during World War II. The message that 'India has emerged on the horizon as an undisputed regional power in South Asia" was transmitted, loud and clear, to the world community.

---

[54] A M Vohra, "Indian Peace Keeping in Sri Lanka", P 94

[55] Air Marshal (Retd) MS Vasudeva, Air Operations.

- **Setbacks and Weaknesses**

  - The IPKF was called upon to essentially fight an infantry war; although the role of other arms and services in support of the infantry have been lauded, that of mechanized forces has been criticized as being too prone to conventional tactics and not being willing to be innovative in the special circumstances of the IPKF's role in Sri Lanka.[56]

  - To be able to send troops to a neighbouring country for policing or for a military operation one has to have a strong and stable government, at least be a mini superpower; be politically and economically strong; have a strong army, air force and a navy with a medium strike radius (something on the lines of the US Seventh Fleet) and be a nuclear power, or atleast have some nuclear capability.[57] India, at the time of induction of IPKF into Sri Lanka had only a few of these pre-requisites.

  - Without being oblivious of the politico-strategic consideration and constraints at the international level, one does feel tempted to think that the induction of IPKF could have been delayed atleast by three to four months which would have given reasonably sufficient time to commanders in planning and training their forces.

  - A word about Indian Amy's naiveté in matters of diplomatic nuances merits attention. The Indian Army is a professional fighting instrument and is not expected to be well versed with the nooks and corners of diplomacy. Apparently the Indian High Commission in Colombo, who had assumed an overbearing role, expected Army to

---

[56] Lt Gen SC Sardeshpande, Assignment Jaffna, pp 139-140.

[57] http://in.rediff.com/news/2000/mar/23lank.

undertake tasks beyond its precincts and outside its values. This was the cause of the 'turf-wars' between the Indian High Commissioner (IHC) and the IPKF.[58]

- There were deficiencies of operational nature that had a direct bearing on the outcome of operations launched by IPKF. The most apparent was the intelligence failure in getting real time and actionable information. This reflected on the intelligence agencies inability to infiltrate the leadership network as well as the ranks of the Tamil Militant groups.

- Excessive reliance on RAW put immense pressure and over-stretched them to provide intelligence, thereby compromising on the quality content.

- Lack of an effective police force in the IPKF's area of operations exacerbated the difficulties of intelligence agencies, (It may be good for the posterity to assimilate and realize that the backbone of the law and order machinery and upward flow of information from grass-root level remains the local police who understands local situation, is familiar with the crime graph and the pattern of operation of criminals and goons, has a documented record of sensitive pockets and suspected miscreants—and therefore, provides the most reliable link for the intelligence agencies).

- Another criticality was 'the weak public relations efforts during the IPKF operations in Sri Lanka'.[59] It led to the failure in seeking public support within India which adversely affected the domestic opinion about the very basis of launching IPKF.

---

[58] Seminar on 'Indian Experience in Force Projection, Chapter II- Change from Peace Keeping to Peace Enforcement '; Maj Gen (Retd) SG Pitre, pp 33.

[59] Lt Gen Depinder Singh, "IPKF in Sri Lanka" pp 192.

- Deficiencies in managing the media in a favourable and propitious manner failed in projecting the IPKF's noble intentions in the minds of Sr Lankan masses. The IPKF's support base therefore kept eroding.

- The IPKF had to fight in an alien country in an unfavourable terrain, face a hostile local populace, fight with little or no intelligence and deal with an unfavourable foreign government who never wanted it (IPKF) in their country in the first place.[60]   Few of these weaknesses could have been offset had there been little more deliberations in an 'integrated domain' prior to the launch of IPKF.

- Certain weaknesses were noticed in the context of higher direction of war also. In this regard late Field Marshal SHFJ Manekshaw had opined, "Despite the obvious professionalism of the Indian Army and its success in anti-insurgency operations in Mizoram, the Fighting Command had too many masters giving different orders and different assessments......."[61]   This concept of 'too many masters giving different orders and different assessments' led to avoidable confusions. It was never clear as to who was drawing up and refining the overall strategy. This unorganized (rather disorganized) and somewhat 'chaotic' and segmented manner of working led to a situation where accountability was diluted and no single authority claimed responsibility for disjointed and piecemeal application of resources. No one seemed to be clear about the overall strategy in Sri Lanka.

- Lack of clear cut and well defined political aim was another important lesson that was learnt during the campaign.

---

[60]   http://in.rediff.com/news/2000/mar/23lank

[61]   SHFJ Manekshaw, in Foreword to Lt Gen Depinder Singh's IPKF in Sri Lanka.

- Budgetary costs and increase in military casualities were other areas of domestic criticism and belief in early withdrawal vis-à-vis any prolonged commitment of IPKF.

While major lessons of the IPKF operations have been brought out in scores of accounts published over the years one of the most significant observation regarding India's first force projection assignment came from none other than Late General K Sundarji who, while speaking at the Third D R Mankekar Memorial Lecture on 13 Feb 1991 said, "India's intervention into Sri Lanka had no national strategy which placed the Commanders and troops in an unacceptable and impossible position. When the government in power took a decision to adopt hard option against the LTTE, it turned out to be a nasty move. The problem could have been avoided if the decision taken had formed part of a well developed National Security Strategy, which the Parliament and People were aware of." It is a universal fact, and perhaps should have been acknowledged by our decision makers, that internal security problems—whether they pertain to law and order, or insurgency, or a terrorist movement — have their roots embedded into the political process. It is incumbent for us to realize therefore that in the absence of a political solution the military instrument of force projection would invariably get blunted, thereby leading to failures and withdrawals. K M de Silva had rightly brought out in his book 'Sri Lanka: Problems of Governance' that, "to be drawn into an ethnic conflict in a neighbouring state is the worst folly for a regional power (no less than for a super power) as Israel and Syria have learned in Lebanon, and India has learned in Sri Lanka."[62] The "folly" of becoming directly involved in the Sri Lankan ethnic conflict is compounded by the fact that India had originally intervened by using Tamil militants to broker a just deal for the Sri Lankan Tamils and thereby preserve, the unity and integrity of Sri Lanka. In hindsight, an early withdrawal of IPKF from Sri Lanka would have prevented an adverse image of India positing in the

---

[62] KM De Silva, Sri Lanka: Problems of Governance", pp 389-90

consciousness of Sri Lankan population. Quite surprisingly, India was fully aware of the problems associated with prolonged occupation of a neighbouring country even though it might have actually been 'invited' to assist that country. This perception and belief was perhaps understood better a few years ago when India opted to a speedy withdrawal from Bangladesh post 1971 lest its defence forces were accused of being an 'occupation force' in that country. The lessons should have been learnt from then-on and IPKF should have been applied for a "shock-effect" rather than being employed as a 'police force' who have all the time to deal with law and order and are rarely "time-bound" to achieve the desired mission.

Lastly, and perhaps most importantly all future 'force projection' operations must be planned and executed in an integrated manner with synergistic application of not only our own force projection components but also of the host nation's armed forces, local police, intelligence agencies and other significant governmental agencies dealing with administration.

Force Projection in Maldives

Maldives, as most of us know is an archipelago in the Indian Ocean and is located 600 kms south west of the Indian mainland. It was in these islands in 1988 that India tasted success in defeating a coup that was staged to oust the Maldivian President Maumoon Abdul Gayoom. Thus, it was the first (and so far the only one) successful attempt at force projection by India which amply demonstrated the willingness of the Indian political leadership to use its military strength in the region to support a friendly regime. The operation was code named as Operation Cactus (OP CACTUS) and was launched on 03 Nov 1988 with Indian Air Force mounting special operations to airlift a Parachute battalion from Agra, non-stop over 2000 km, out beyond the south-western coast of India to the remote Indian Ocean islands of Maldives. In response to the Maldivian Government's appeal for military help against a mercenary invasion the IL-76s of Indian Air Force landed at Halule airport at 0030 hours. The Indian paratroopers secured the airfield and restored Government rule at Male within hours. Buildup of forces continued the next day, with IL-76s, AN-12s and AN-32s flown to Maldives from Trivandrum, while Mirage 2000s made low level passes over the scattered islands in a show of force. The most immediate reality that emerged from this brief and bloodless action was the swift and effective military response, made possible by the IAF's strategic airlift capability.[63] Within hours, some 1600 Indian troops were dispatched who, over the course of next three days, rounded up the mercenaries involved in the attempted coup and successfully restored the situation in the host country; thus establishing India's credibility as a regional power. The Indian Navy played an equally significant role in blocking the escape routes that the coup leaders might have exploited to make their escape good. It was truly an integrated and jointly accomplished mission that was collectively executed by the three services.

Lessons Learnt in Maldives Operations

Maldives chapter undisputedly was a success story all the way; but to sit on the success without introspection and critical analysis may prove counter-productive. Wise men are those who learn from successes as well as failures, without getting reverentially awed by the former or abhorrently disgusted by latter. OP CACTUS gave us adequate lessons to ponder and 'work on' for ensuring smooth conduct of future force projection operations. Some of these lessons are:-

- **Positives**

    - Quick political decision that led to prompt convening of the Cabinet Committee on Political Affairs and consequent approval for military intervention. It may be appropriate to analyse the under mentioned time

---

[63]   http://indianairforce.nic.in/show-page.php?Pg-id=109

schedule to get a better perspective of the speed in decision making and equally fast response in implementation of the political direction:-[64]

o **03 Nov 1988**

-**5.30 AM:** Maldive's Minister of Foreign Affairs called Shri Rajiv Gandhi and requested Indian assistance to quell the coup.

- **7.30 AM**: Three ILs 76 aircrafts placed on a "Stand By-Three Hours" notice in Agra. Almost at same time, 50 (Indep) Parachute Brigade was also issued the Warning Order for move.

-**9 AM**: Cabinet Committee on Political Affairs (CCPA) was convened.

- **10 AM**: Squadron at Agra was ready with the three aircrafts.The Parachute Brigade had also started its Battle Procedure for the impending Task (that was not yet disclosed).

- **1.30 PM:** The CCPA gave approval for the military support.

-**3 PM** : 50(Indep) Parachute Brigade had mobilized.

- **3.30 PM**: The first three aircrafts with crew of 44 Sqn and Vanguard of Parachute Brigade were ready for the launch.

- **3.45PM:** Team of Officers from the Army and Air HQs arrived from New Delhi with definite information and crucial inputs. The team was

---

[64] Group Captain (Retd) AG Bewoor, VM; "OP CACTUS: Reminiscences", (Extracts only).

accompanied by the Indian High Commissioner to Maldives, Mr Banerjee who was coincidentally   in Delhi when the attempted coup was being staged in Maldives.

- 5.45PM: Refueling of aircrafts was completed in a record time - a feat that was unprecedented in the history of Indian Air Force.

- 6.04PM: First aircraft took-off from Agra.

- 9.25PM: First Radio/Tele contact was established with the Halule Airport after   which   the Landing commenced.

- 10.20 PM: Complete island of Halule was secured by troops.

o **04 Nov 1988**

- 2.15AM: By now President Gayoom was under the protection of Parachute Brigade.

- 4 AM : High Commissioner of India Mr Banerjee and Brig FFC Balsara met the Maldivian President.

Note: Thereafter the sanitization of the area and mopping up operations continued over the next two days and the task force returned to India on 06 Nov 1988.

- The Indian Navy launched a surgical operation in intercepting the terrorists on high seas. The terrorists killed one hostage but surrendered to INSs Godavari and Betwa. They were brought back to Male along with all hostages. The entire operation was an example of a fine naval engagement with good lessons to imbibe from.

- Our capability to react swiftly, assertively and with firm resolve and determination was successfully demonstrated to the world community.

- It was the first instance of a truly integrated response by most, if not all elements of comprehensive national power that included following:-

    - Political set up and leadership

    - Diplomatic support (Indian High Commissioner to Maldives was himself an active member of the Task Force.)

    - Indian Defence Forces

    - Responsible media reporting

    - Favourable public opinion

- Reasonable degree of surprise and deception was achieved during the entire operation.

- A very high degree of communication security and radio silence contributed immensely in the overall success of the operation.

- A totally integrated and truly synergistic approach assayed the successful culmination of the assigned task.

- Significance of rehearsals was not lost sight of; and therefore utmost use of available time was made even at the Agra airfield when troops were rehearsing while plans were being crystallized in consultation with the Team of officers from Delhi.

- Leading by example was amply demonstrated by officers of all arms and services.

- Initiative and actions without waiting for orders resulted in quick responses at all levels.

- Speed in induction as well as orientation was another important hallmark of the entire operation.

- **Areas of Concern**

  - The weakest link in the entire operation was intelligence. There were glaring deficiencies in terms of voids in crucial inputs and flow of information. Even the basic maps of the area were not available.

  - Database needs to be built, atleast in respect of our neighbouring countries wherein all the necessary inputs should be docketed. It may be interesting to note that the Task Force earmarked for OP CACTUS had no knowledge about the Halule Runway where the landing was to be executed. Ironically enough, Indian Airlines had been operating flights to Halule, and therefore, an Indian Airlines Pilot who had flown early could have been brought to Agra for briefing the crew and to accompany them on board. Even 'Doordarshan had a video recording of Halule Runway taken during the SAARC Summit in April 1988 which was telecast on National TV at 2130hrs on 03 Nov 88, just 15 minutes before K-2878 landed at Halule'.

  - A Rapid Deployment Force (RDF) comprising elements of all three Services be raised and co-located at places from where they can be launched with minimum loss of time.

  - Concept of issue of Joint Warning Order be evolved to obviate the possibility of voids and gaps with regards to crucial inputs that need to be provided to troops earmarked for impending task.

- Compatibility of weapons and equipment to ensure smooth launch and induction.

- Sound and secure communication network be evolved and rehearsed by all components of the Task Force likely to be earmarked for OOA and EBO operations.

- Principle of centralized control and decentralized execution be followed.[65]

Operation Cactus at Halule was India's first strategic intervention that was undertaken based on a bilateral understanding between two regional states[66]. The fact that the operation was flawlessly executed with professional élan and conviction was acknowledged by the world powers who watched the events as mute spectators. Audaciously daring and swift response to a neighbour's call for assistance though was honoured promptly but only after a considered decision by the political masters gave the green signal to the military intervention. Lastly and most importantly, we may conclude with awe and sense of utmost satisfaction that our first 'strategic intervention and force projection' attempt was successful but we must not lose sight of the fact that so much could have gone wrong; and so much did actually go wrong. The lessons therefore need to be analysed in correct perspective and should serve as a sounding board for meticulousness in all spheres of planning and execution for all future assignments of similar nature.

---

[65] Proceedings of Seminar on Indian Experience in Force Projection conducted by CENJOWS on 15-16 Sept 2008; Maldives Operations pp 168.

[66] ibid, pp 168.

CHAPTER 7

INTEGRATED FORCE PROJECTION BY INDIA

*Before you start some work, always ask yourself three questions -
Why am I doing it, what the results might be and will I be successful.
Only when you think deeply and find satisfactory answers to these
questions, go ahead.*

- Kautilya

India, a nation that emerged from the colonial rules by showcasing
the power of Gandhian non-violence, continued to follow the path of
"peace" and 'non-interference' even in its post independence 'avatar'
and did not harbour any hegemonistic ambitions. It derided the force
projection tendencies of the developed world and focused itself on
the policy of self-defence primarily against the two neighbours, China
and Pakistan. However, the developments over the past few decades
in terms of newer strategic alliances, emergence of a new world
order and belligerently defiant, pugnacious and bellicose tendencies
of some of the nation states have forced India to shed its inward
looking mindset. The Indian polity, having the strength, resilience
and experience of many centuries decided to respond to these rising
manifestations of power politics in international relations and refashion
India into a regional power with global reach. Today, "India sees itself
in a different light — not looking so much inward or merely looking at
Pakistan, but globally", said William Cohen, Secretary of Defence in
the Clinton administration. He further added, "India's sending a signal

that it's going to be a big player." These observations get corroborated by what the then Prime Minister Vajpayee had conveyed to the strategic think tanks and planners in Nov 2002 when he directed them 'to craft defence strategies that extend beyond South Asia and transcend past sub-regional mindsets. India's expanded security perspectives, he claimed; require fresh thinking about projecting power and influence, as well as security in all these directions. The message clearly signalled that India had graduated to the status of asserting itself as a global player with aspirations of being a regional power in and around Asia and the IOR. Major policy decisions, such as the one to go overtly nuclear in 1998, can be attributed to this consuming desire to be seen as a great power. For years, both, Indian and Foreign analysts have expected that by the early 21st Century India would become a major projector of power and influence throughout Asia. Indeed, the most recent evidence suggests that the government has opted for a 20 year programme to fulfil that goal and "become a world power with influence spreading across the Indian Ocean, the Arabian Gulf and the four corners of Asia."[67]

Translating these ideas and thoughts into reality necessitate that India should get its political, diplomatic, military and economic act together. The young parliamentarian Rahul Gandhi had once said in one of his speeches in the Parliament in 2009, "What is important is that we stop getting worried about how the world will impact us, we stop being scared about how the world will affect us, and rather step out and worry about how will we impact the world." Presently India's national security policy operates at two levels, firstly at the political and diplomatic levels and secondly, on the military prowess. At the politico-diplomatic levels we are engaging our neighbours through peace proposals and negotiations. We are successfully managing and resolving conflicts and enhancing national interests through non-military means. Notwithstanding that, we need to acknowledge that maintaining peace and stability with our neighbours in the region,

[67] Stephen Blank, 'India's Grand Strategic Vision Gets Grander', Asia Times Online Ltd; 2003.

and even in the global context, through diplomacy would be effective only if it (diplomacy) is backed by credible military deterrence and by maintaining armed forces at the highest levels of defence preparedness with ability to react and project force swiftly. Even the global and regional scan highlights that we need to shed our inward looking and reactive sub-continental mindset. The strategic frontiers of India therefore would extend beyond the conventionally perceived physical borders which necessitate that India has to strive to be both, a Maritime as well as a Continental Power with adequate resources to undertake force projection operations.

Strategic Concerns of India

The Strategic Concerns of India can thus be envisaged as a set of concentric circles as shown in the figure on the next page. The innermost circle encompasses China, Pakistan and other smaller neighbours that share the land or maritime boundaries namely, Bhutan, Bangladesh, Myanmar, Sri Lanka, Maldives and Nepal. The internal stability of these states is a burgeoning concern for us since any instability would call for increased border security and *in extremis* ability to project regional force at a very short notice as was done in Maldives in 1988.[68] This therefore necessitates that a Rapid Reaction Force must be readily available for such Force Projection Operations.

Closer home, China continues to be one of the major adversarial competitors for India — not merely against the backdrop of a conventional war but also because of its increasingly fancied interests in our immediate neighbourhood of Nepal, Bhutan and Myanmar, and more importantly in the Indian Ocean Region. While India's recent approach has been to facilitate slow reconciliation, accentuate new opportunities and downplay controversies plaguing Sino-Indian relations, it does not augur well for India to ignore the reality that China, of late, has been pursuing the policy of 'string of pearls' which

---

[68] John H Gill, India and Pakistan. A shift in the Military Calculus, Strategic Asia, 2005-06, pp 238.

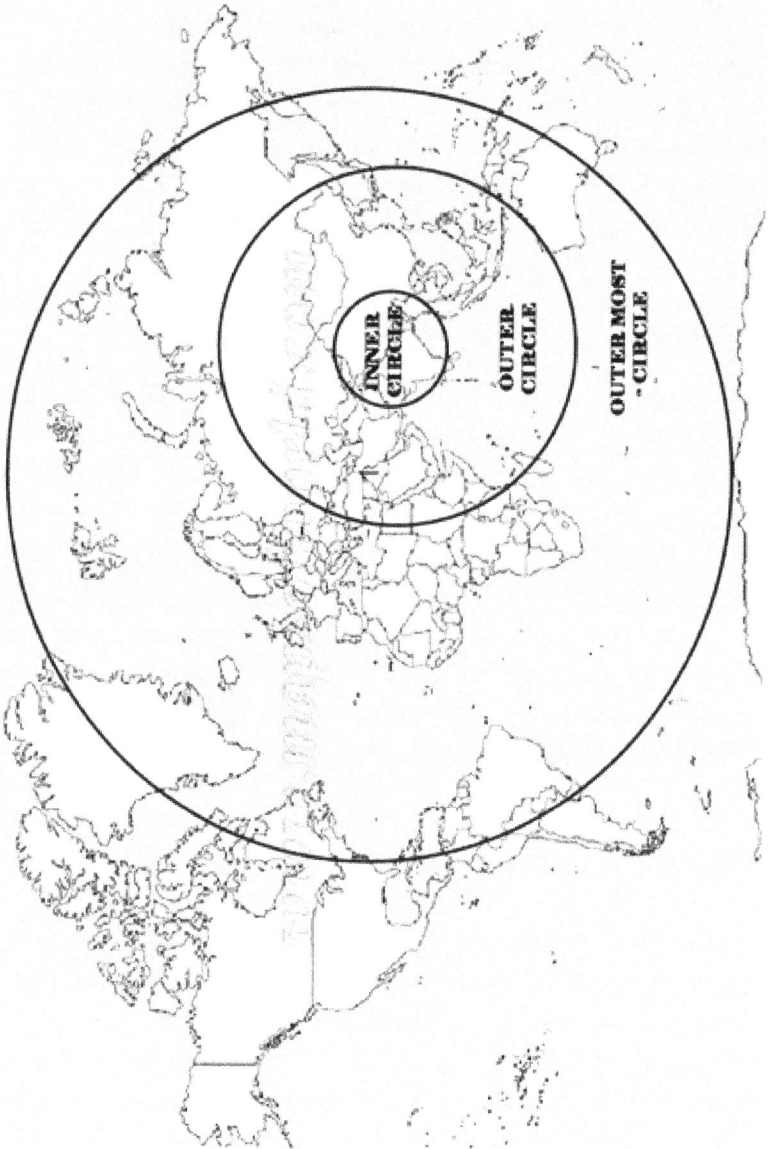

STRATEGIC CONCERNS OF INDIA

will have a direct implication on our maritime security. The need, therefore, of having a suitable naval complement to undertake force projection operations in the Indian Ocean Region has to be accorded utmost priority.

Similarly, an anatomical analysis of Indo-Pak relations since independence reveals that the relations have been punctuated with conventional wars and conflicts including Kargil misadventure by Pakistan in 1991, a near-war confrontation during 'Operation Parakram' in 2001-02, routine artillery duals till 2003 and the blatantly unrelenting Pakistani support to the fundamentalist divisive forces in Kashmir ever since independence. Therefore, a possible direct or indirect assistance by Pakistan to stoke separatism in the Indian littoral region as well as in the smaller neighbouring states like Bhutan, Nepal, Maldives etc necessitates the requirement of a suitably located, well rehearsed and ready to launch force to undertake force projection operations in these areas.

The next circle of policy concern for New Delhi includes the Persian Gulf, Central Asia and South East Asia. With over 70 percent of India's oil drawn from the Gulf, and an expectation that demand will rise dramatically in the coming decades, India has a vital interest in the maintenance of stability in Iran and the Arabian Gulf states. Furthermore, an estimated 3.5 million Indians work in the Gulf, providing valuable remittances and obligating New Delhi to take their safety into consideration.[69] Iran is also important as a potential avenue for commercial access to Central Asia and Afghanistan. Good relations with all these countries coupled with a demonstrated resolve to intervene with an appropriate force, ordain a very high degree of preparedness at all times, thereby necessitating suitably grouped, equipped and well rehearsed projection force readily available for launch at short notice.

---

[69] Indian Ministry of Defence, Annual Report 2004-05, pp13.

The outermost circle of India's security interests encompasses global issues and interactions with more distant governments, chiefly the United States. In this arena, New Delhi recognizes that broad and deep ties with the world's sole super power are central to India's continued economic success and to what Indian leaders see as the recovery of India's due status in the world.[70] However, while maintaining a close proximity and good diplomatic relations with US, India will have to ensure that it continues to maintain healthy and friendly relations with countries like Russia, UK, France, Brazil, South Africa etc lest it is christened as an undeclared ally of the United States. Furthermore, New Delhi has to realize that it can attain a regional power status only when it announces a declared force projection doctrine and projects itself as a politically strong, militarily credible, diplomatically wise, internally stable and an economically sound nation state.

Need for Credible Force Projection Capability

All these areas, coupled with following geo-strategic realities gives rise to the need for having a credible force projection capability for the country:-

- The peninsular identity of the geographical landmass implies larger EEZ and claim lines into the IOR which necessitates the requirement of having suitable force projection capability.

- Manifestations of fundamentalist groups in the last few decades pose threat to the littoral regions as well as in the immediate neighbourhood.

- Sheer size of the nation imposes heavy reliance on its shoulders for providing an inherent sense of security to its smaller neighbours in South Asia.

---

[70] John H Gill, India and Pakistan: A Shift in the Military Calculus,pp 241.

- Positive demand for Indian presence both in the East and the Middle East. The demand comes from those nations who see Indian power as benign and counter-weight against unwanted hegemony by certain global players. 'In the East, Singapore with its fuelling agreement for the Navy and an annual strategic dialogue is a willing gateway for Indian power. In the West, the smaller Gulf States are desperate for an Indian presence provided it is large and strong to be of significance. In the South Indian Ocean where the distances are large, we see deep inroads by China into Mauritius.[71] It has invariably been seen that China follows a well calculated and time tested method of asserting its projection capabilities in a phased manner—it first establishes trade relations and consolidates it through subsidies and preferential agreements, thereafter enters the domestic market through infrastructural development and civil construction in that country and finally, ices the power projection cake with strategic partnerships and covert or overt presence in the host nation territory. Examples of this intent are many; but to name a few, we have Chinese stakes in infrastructural development in Myanmar, construction of Hambantota Port in Sri Lanka and Gwadar port in Pakistan. While "aping" and "copying" these ideas and methodology will not benefit India in any manner, taking a 'cue' from these developments and evoking fresh strategy on these lines may not be a bad option for our own force projection intentions.

- India's growing energy needs will impose immense reliance on its Navy to provide security for unimpeded access to oil, thus necessitating our presence along the SLOCs and vulnerable choke points in international waters.

---

[71] Robert D Kaplan, Power Plays in the Indian Ocean, Foreign Affairs, Mar/Apr 2009.

- New Delhi has realized that an expanding menu of international military interactions has enhanced India's status and acceptance as a major player in the regional dynamics as well as at the global stage. The corollary therefore is that India must strengthen its force projection capabilities to cope with the pressures and expectations of being a dominant power.

India's Recent Force Projection Signatures

Force Projection is often misconstrued and misinterpreted as demonstration of military muscle without realizing that military is just one of the components of force projection; it is merely a means to attain the desired national goal of projecting a nation's comprehensive national power. Over the years, India's force projection signatures have also been acquiesced and homologated by the world community, thus exponentially enhancing India's status as regional power suitably equipped with various tools in its force projection inventory.

Some of the successful force projection ventures undertaken by India need to be taken note of so as to serve as benchmarks for future preparations and formulation of force projection policies and doctrines. These are:-

- Besides Maldives and Sri Lanka, which have already been discussed in the previous chapter, India had demonstrated its resolve to intervene in Mauritius in 1980s. However, the threat passed off and India never descended on Mauritian soil but the intent had been conveyed to the world that India would not hesitate to project its forces if the situation demanded so.

- Indian blockade of Nepal by Rajiv Gandhi government in 1989-90 over a dispute consequent to Chinese interference. The blockade led to the King appointing a Prime Minister who was sympathetic towards India.[72] One of the UN studies has quoted it as one of the most decisive blockades to change state behaviour. This is an obvious indicator of the political set up that has the capability and will to undertake force projection whenever national interests demand so.

- In 1992, Indian Navy had constantly undertaken surveillance and patrolling tasks off Somalian Coast as part of the UN's multinational force under 'Operation Restore Hope'. In addition, our army contingent also participated under the aegis of UN in Somalia and projected our intentions of sending the armed forces for restoring peace and normalcy.

- When Tsunami struck in December 2004, Indian Air Force air lifted over 2300 tonnes of relief material and rescued over 55000 passengers.[73] This was an unprecedented act by any air force in such a short time frame indicative of our prompt response capabilities. Similarly, Indian Navy was the first to rush aid to Maldives, Sri Lanka and Indonesia which were hit the worst by Tsunami. About 1000 Indian relief personnel and five naval ships were sent to Trincomalee, Galle and Colombo Ports in Sri Lanka with medical teams and immediate relief material. Total naval commitment during Tsunami, according to news accounts, was 16,000 troops, 32 warships, 41 planes and a floating hospital. The fact that India could deploy its navy within 24 hours of Tsunami created ripples throughout the world.

- The IAF's peace keeping operations in Congo and Sudan in 2005-06 won international accolades. Similarly, numerous

---

[72] Gary Hufbauer and Kemberley Eliot, Economic Sanctions Reconsidered (Institute for International Economics: Washington) 2nd Edition, 1990.

[73] NISDA Security Conference 2005; Inaugural Address and Gen BC Joshi Memorial Lecture on "Role of the IAF in the Changing Regional Security Environment", Air Chief Marshal (Retd) SP Tyagi, PVSM, AVSM, VSM.

other peace keeping operations undertaken by Army have successfully projected India's military potential.

- During the Israel-Lebanon Conflict in 2006, the Indian Navy sent warships to evacuate 2,280 Lebanese, Sri Lankan and Nepalese citizens besides 700 Indians. Contrastingly, few decades ago the nation would have merely watched thousands of Indians in jeopardy in a foreign land and might have reconciled that there was nothing their military could do.

- The Indian Navy's 'proactive' move against Somali pirates in the strategic Gulf of Aden in November 2008 marks a significant step in India's aspirations of projecting its force beyond its borders. The robust response by INS Tabar in sinking a pirate vessel in a retaliatory fire almost 3000 kms away from its home port of Mumbai has reiterated the credibility of Indian Navy in force projection thereby signalling a paradigm shift in the power projection of the Indian Navy which was, thus far, considered only as a defensive force guarding its 5514 km coastline. In pursuit of its newfound role of force projection, Indian Navy is acquiring the bigger symbols of potent maritime force in the aircraft carriers and nuclear submarines.

Paradigm Shift in India's Force Projection Outlook

India's transformational forays and military modernization initiatives have brought it closer to its grand strategic goals of building a force projection capability. Today, it acquiesces that a robust military is vital for cementing its claims as a regional power that possesses the teeth to project itself whenever geo-political necessity warrants demonstration of such a resolve. "Ten years from now, India could be a real provider of security to all 'the islands in the Indian Ocean," said Ashley Tellis, an Indian born scholar at the Carnegie Endowment for International Peace in Washington. He further stated, "It could become a provider of security in the Persian Gulf in collaboration with the US. I would think of the same being true with the Central Asian States." "India", he added, "is slowly maturing into a conventional great power."

While India formally eschews offensive military projection, it has formally announced its base in Tajikistan, and hopes to undertake the following military programme through 2013:-

- Improve military logistics in Iran, Tajikistan, Kazakhstan and Uzbekistan.

- Increase military interaction with Malaysia, Indonesia, Singapore, Thailand, Laos and Vietnam.

- Increase naval interaction with South Africa, other African States, Iran, Oman, the UAE and other Gulf nations.

- Extend infrastructure, logistic and material support to Myanmar to contain Chinese activities there.

- Buy armaments that major powers like the United States and NATO had been using thus far. Some of these systems include aircraft carriers C-130J Hercules transporters, air-to-air Refuellers like IL-78s, aerostats, satellite systems etc.[74]

- India also appears to be positioning itself as a caretaker and patroller of the Indian Ocean Region.

- The Indian Air Force (IAF), benefiting from steady growth in its share of the defense budget since 2001, has been making important acquisitions that will effectively support its Out of Area Contingency operations. The heart of IAF's modernization is the acquisition of key force multipliers in terms of air-to-air tankers i.e. IL-78s, which have significantly

---

[74] Stephen Blank, "India's Grand Strategic Vision Gets Grander," Asia Time Online Ltd, 2003.

enhanced the loiter time and range of many of its fighter aircrafts. Similarly, inclusion of AWACS in its inventory has been a major achievement for the IAF. Of the three services, Indian Navy's modernization efforts have the potential for the broadest strategic applicability. The Navy's greatest concern is China, but New Delhi's maritime calculations also encompass such security issues as piracy, drug trafficking and interdiction of terrorists.[75]

- The Maritime Doctrine announced in 2004 specifically calls for the Indian Navy to serve as an "effective instrument of foreign policy," not only as a source of coercive military power, but also as a diplomatic link to other countries.[76]

- The Navy's plan to build a force of three carriers is underway. This would ensure a 'round the clock' availability of two Carrier Battle Groups which would strengthen India's force projection capabilities.

Transformational Dynamics

Force projection operations necessitate launching Effect Based and Out of Area Contingency Operations. Both these variants, like any other military operation, depend upon three dimensions namely policy formulation, issue of vision statement and close integration between all operational modules. The transformational dynamics will have to take into account the impact of all these dimensions before working out the structural modules for the force being earmarked to undertake integrated force projection operations. The force structure will have to respond to the dynamics of national interests, and therefore, will have to remain bound by the policy guidelines and political directives that define our strategic vision. The key challenges that would govern

[75] New Naval Doctrine: Stresses on Developing Nuclear Triad Outlook, June 23, 2004.

[76] Indian Navy, Indian Maritime Doctrine (2004), pp102.

evolution of the requisite structure for force projection operations would be:-

- Formulation of long-term policy guidelines with legitimate and *dejure* avenues for free and frank politico-military exchange on strategic issues that affect our national interests. Participation in politico-military strategizing on likely global and regional crises scenarios should be encouraged.

- Vision statement to clearly define responsibilities of various components of Comprehensive National Power, both, at the apex level as well as at the functional domain.

- Closer integration between all operational modules.

- Consummately entwined and interlaced foreign policy guidelines, geo-strategic interests and national objectives.

- Frictionless, synchronized and integrated intelligence set up.

- Flatter organizational structure with minimal vertices.

- Sustained focus on integrated training to achieve superlative preparedness in launching force projection operations.

- Information Warfare to be treated as a command function and not a mere staff function.

- Preclude adhocism in working out force composition.

- Enunciate integrated doctrine and address the issue of 'institutional resistance to change' with a deliberately carved out strategy for improving inter-agency and inter-service coordination.

- Defence Procurement Procedures need to be diluted without compromising the built-in regulatory mechanism.

- Robust, sinewy and multi-spectral logistic set up with built in redundancy to ensure uninterrupted supply chain management for sustaining the force projection operations.

Finally, concerted diplomatic efforts will have to be undertaken to forge mutually beneficial partnerships in the strategic, economic and technological spheres aimed at enlarging our strategic outreach through force projection options.

Force Projection Vision for India

India's emergence as a global player has been amply demonstrated in recent times. In fact, it can easily boast of its newly acquired credentials and leverage its politico-military by-product, suitably backed by the economic consolidation, to stake its legitimate claims to the title of a Regional Power. In this regard it may be appropriate to cite a recent example of our diplomatic success in Sri Lanka on the issue of setting up of an Expert Group by UN to assess accountability (post demise of LTTE). Sri Lanka supported its defiant attitude against establishment of an Experts Panel by UN on the issue of internally Displaced Persons (IDPs) by quoting the statement made by Indian Foreign Secretary Nirupama Rao during her visit to Sri Lanka in second week of March 2010. She had reportedly stated, "Sri Lanka had made considerable success in resettling IDPs and this issue had now gone away from the attention of international community." This news was carried by the Daily Mirror in its March 08, 2010 edition Sri Lanka government as well as Sri Lankan media highlighted this statement to convey to the UN that the issue of IDP is now a non-issue in view of the 'assertion coming from an international diplomat (Indian Foreign Secretary) whose credentials surpass those of experts sent by the UN.' The comment is clearly impregnated with an eloquently encapsulated triumph for the Indian diplomacy and elevates India to the pedestal of regional power fiefdom. In order to tread this course of ascendancy to the ladder of power we need to work towards strengthening our security alliances with other international actors and regional players. There is no harm in taking a cue from the United States' doctrine of 'Pre-emptive Intervention' which provides her the opportunity to create pressure points and enforce, engage or intervene militarily when other options fail. Aping this concept blindly will certainly amount to foolhardiness, especially in the backdrop of our national policy of 'non-interference in the internal affairs of other nations'. However, a dexterously worked out model of stepping-in to address such regional contingencies and crises that may have a direct affect on our geo-strategic interests can certainly be worked out.

A deliberately thought out force projection strategy therefore needs to be formulated in consonance with our continental and maritime aspirations. To achieve such strategic ambitions our military capabilities will have to be increased significantly, both in terms of transformational changes as well as review of our force structure. The same has been explained with the help of a Figure that highlights the following attributes of such a projection force:-

- Fully integrated

- Reliance on inter-operability

- Harmony and Synergy in inter-agency and intra-agency functioning

- Net Centricity and technological driven

- Quick response & speed in launching the missions

- Ability to generate desired effects in minimum time

- Sound Mechanism to undertake periodic review of all bilateral ties and agreements within the region as well as in the global dimension

- Ensure evolution of a frictionless and perceivably just and common hierarchical set up that should focus on broader national objectives and overlook narrow parochial domains

EVOLUTION OF FORCE PROJECTION STRATEGY

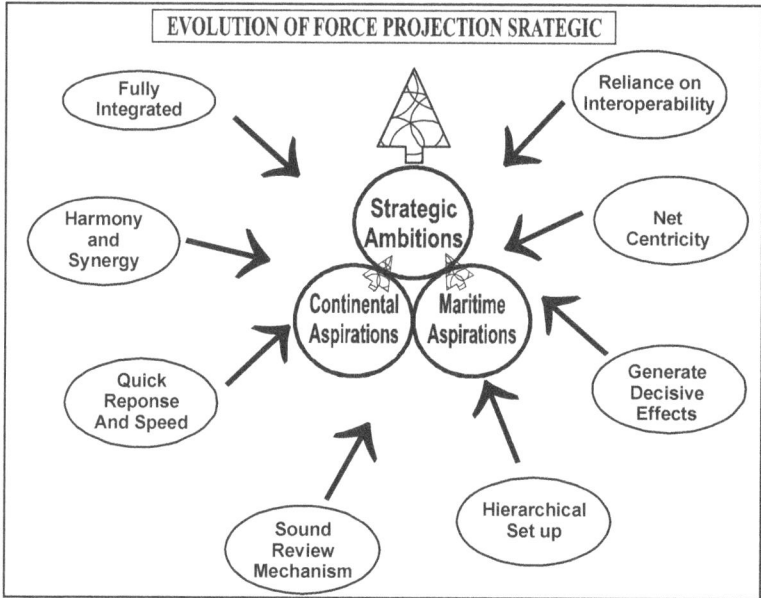

Areas of Focus for Force Projection

The foremost requirement for developing a credible force to undertake force projection missions is to de-hyphenate this concept from the concept of defence of the nation. The precipitate thought that force projection is one of the tasks of our defence forces alone will have to be succinctly erased from the cerebral storehouses of the nation. The causal relationship of force projection with all elements of Comprehensive National Power will have to be studied in detail to conjure up and stimulate our policy makers for stirring up prolific germinative ideas that would enable us to evolve a sound Force Projection Doctrine for the nation. Some of the areas that merit focus in this regard have been shown with the help of a figure and have been explained below:-

- **Change of Mindset**

  This is the most challenging task for the country since we, as a nation, have to learn to have "faith and belief" in our own capabilities. In order to be recognized as a regional power we ought to convey, albeit diplomatically through our policies, that we are prepared for unilateral politico-military intervention in the region as and when we smell any threat to our national interests.

  While unilateral military intervention intent is being announced to the world, India's willingness to participate in UN Peace Keeping missions should also be pursued as hitherto fore. Similarly, military to military cooperation and bilateral/ multilateral military exercises must also continue.

- **Political Vision**

  A long term political vision needs to be evolved and vigorously pursued beyond petty party lines and personality driven policies. Either an all party conclave or a deliberate parliamentary debate may have to be planned to define the

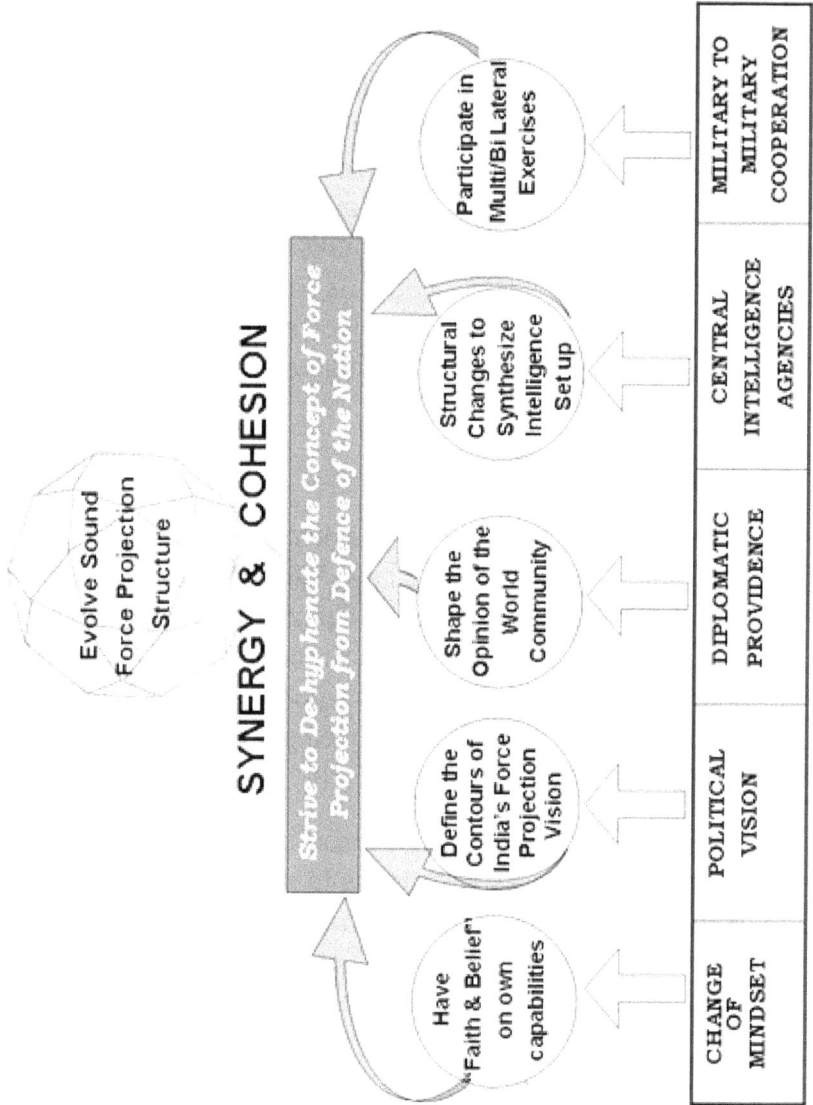

SYNERGY & COHESION

Strive to Dehyphenate the Concept of Force Projection from Defence of the Nation

Evolve Sound Force Projection Structure

Participate in Multi/Bi Lateral Exercises

Structural Changes to Synthesize Intelligence Set up

Shape the Opinion of the World Community

Define the Contours of India's Force Projection Vision

Have "Faith & Belief" on own capabilities

| CHANGE OF MINDSET | POLITICAL VISION | DIPLOMATIC PROVIDENCE | CENTRAL INTELLIGENCE AGENCIES | MILITARY TO MILITARY COOPERATION |

contours of India's Force Projection Vision at least till 2050. This would pave the way for bureaucracy and the strategic community to work out a broad framework on which the country's Force Projection Doctrine can be based.

- **Diplomatic Providence**

  Our diplomacy, possibly, faces the most daunting task of "shaping the opinion" of the world community, especially so, in our immediate neighbourhood. It needs to efface and erase the dubious distinction of India being seen as a "big-brother" in the region. The deviously deceitful, sneaky and furtively accomplished designs of some of our neighbours in projecting India as a 'big-brother' need to be dexterously annulled and negated by our diplomacy. Our stature as a regional power will consolidate only if our neighbours are convinced that India considers them as "equals" and would always respect their identity and sovereignty. Their pre-conceived notion and predicated belief of 'big-brother syndrome' will have to be supplanted by the concept of equality through a deft and subtle diplomatic effort. Only then, can we hope of recognition as a regional power based on our national policies and geo-strategic reality.

- **Central Intelligence Agency**

  National Security Council is the pivotal governmental agency for all strategic planning in the country. However, there is a need to have a focused approach with regards to an effective control over plethora of intelligence agencies operating both, at the centre and the state levels. The sprawling bureaucracy and reluctance to share actionable intelligence have to give way to the concept of synergy and collective approach. Our diplomatic missions abroad will have to gear up to evolve a database that would enable the projection force to plan its intended operations based on these inputs. Structural changes may have to be worked out to synthesize and evolve an intelligence set up that could be relied upon, in toto.

- **Review of the Organizational Structure**

The fabric of force projection needs proper care and darning. It cannot have the requisite shine and sheen unless a deliberate thought is given to preserve its texture that binds it together and provides the strength to last longer. Concurrent with modernization of defence forces and Revolution in Military Affairs (RMA), force projection necessitates a similar Revolution in Civil Affairs (RCA) since some of the structural components of civil set up will play a determining role in the successful outcome of force projection operations. Currently, the National Security Council (NSC) is the principal body looking after the all encompassing dimensions of national security. It has a three tiered structure comprising Strategic Policy Group (SPG), the National Security Advisory Board (NSAB) and a secretariat to provide the requisite secretarial support. The NSC is a deliberative body which supports the Cabinet Committee on Security (CCS) and the Cabinet Committee on Parliamentary Affairs (CCPA) in security decision making. The Cabinet Secretariat Resolution No 281/ 29.6.98/TS dated 16 April 1999 announcing the creation of NSC stated, "The Central Government recognizes that national security management requires integrated thinking and coordinated application of the political, military, diplomatic, scientific and technological resources of the state to protect and promote national security goals and objectives. National security, in the context of the nation, needs to be viewed not only in military terms but also in terms of internal security, economic security, technological strength and foreign policy. The role of the council is to advice the Central Government on the said matters."[77]

---

[77] Sainik Samachar, 01 Feb 2001; Challenges to Indian Security-III (Also available at the website http://mod.nic.in/Samachar/1Feb01/html/splash.htm

The charter gives sweeping powers to the NSC and authorizes it to deal comprehensively with all dimensions and manifestations of national security. It is mandated to address internal and external issues traditionally associated with security, intelligence coordination and diplomatic management of the national interests. Thus, it is obviously clear that the gamut of power projection— both hard power as well as soft power, falls very much into the charter of NSC and therefore, it must leverage the country's potential to enable it to project its power in the region. Unfortunately, this system is not able to fumigate and purify our rusty functional set up which prevents it from opening its door to all the essentially important and indispensable components of security network in the country. Dr Subhash Kapila, an eminent security analyst had summarized some of the key shortcomings in the NSC system. These are:-

- Lack of direct access to the political leadership.

- Duplication of the functions of NSA, thereby denying   full time attention to the NSC.

- The NSAB should preferably comprise experienced policy makers and analysts from a wide variety of disciplines to include external affairs, defence, home, commerce, economy, information technology, environment and so on to make it representative of the current security concerns. As it has 32 members there is ample scope for including sufficient number of members from diverse fields.[78]

Since, we are focused more on the aspect of Force Projection, it would be apt to confine and limit the recommendations to only those changes in the structure that will have a direct implication for India's force projection intent. Some of these changes therefore, could be:-

---

[78] Dr Subhash Kapila, "India's National Security Council: A Critical Review," South Asia Analysis Group, 10 May 2005.

- Have a separate cell within the NSC which should be dedicated for following tasks:-

  - Out of Area Contingencies.

  - Hard as well as Soft Power Projection by India.

  - Humanitarian aid.

  - Disaster Relief.

- Incorporate representatives of the key agencies that are dealing with intelligence network, both within and outside the country. This should include RAW, IB and DIA representatives.

- The three Service Chiefs (or Vice Chiefs) should be 'on board' the NSC flagship.

- Besides the traditional players in national security (External Affairs, Defence, Home and Finance) the following should also be associated with force projection planning and execution process:

  - Information and Broadcasting (To ensure responsible and productive media coverage of all force projection operations).

  - Cultural Affairs Ministry (To dovetail Soft Power Projection alongside the hard option).

  - Industries and Commerce Ministry (To provide necessary support to the Force Projection commander for infrastructural development and rehabilitation process after successful conduct of Out of Area Contingency Operations in the host nation's territory).

  - Non Governmental Organisations (NGOs) can also have a salient role in perception management in the host country, i.e. target area where force projections operations are launched. It is time to institutionalize a system wherein

NGOs can contribute immensely in achieving favourable outcome for the Out of Area Contingency and Effect Based Operations. These NGOs can provide assistance in providing humanitarian aids, strengthening health services, boosting infrastructural development, supporting rebuilding process etc.

- Information age has exponentially impacted all dimensions of national security as well as our day to day life. The force multiplier potential of the information technology, communication and media proliferation has to be remuneratively exploited. The very principle of "need to know" on which information sharing was based in the three defence forces has to give way to the concept of "responsibility to provide information". Thus, in view of adequacy in terms of information technology tools available to the government, and to various other agencies, it would be possible to supplement the force projection components and contingents with suitably vetted, validated, and sifted information prior to the launch, during and after the conduct of force projection operations.

Proposed Structure: Key Requirements for Integration.

To meet internal and external challenges to the state and the citizenry, security sector reforms in the contemporary context include a wide range of activities and involve a number of organizations[79]. Similarly, the force projection dimension also necessitates a joint structure that would include numerous important role players ranging from Ministerial representatives, intelligence agencies, military component, supply chain management system, media representation and scores of other supplements. The challenge would be to create an

---

[79] Susanna Bearne, Olga Oliker, Kevin A O 'Brien, Andrew Rathmell, National Security Decision Making Structures and Security Sector Reforms, Prepared for the United Kingdoms Security Sector Development Advisory Team, RAND 2005 (Available at www.dfid.gov.uk/Pubs/files/security- decision-making.pdf

interlocking structure that would ensure a seamless integration of all these components. Key requirements for such an integration process would entail:-

- Special cell in National Security Council that should deal with out of area contingencies including disaster management. This cell should provide significant and timely advice and recommendations to the Prime Minister (through Cabinet Committee on Security and National Security Council).

- Regular interaction amongst the Ministries that have a stake in the force projection process. Periodicity of interaction and sharing of information should be clearly defined.

- A periodic review of threat assessments duly integrating inputs from all agencies should be carried out. Dissemination should be carried out through the 'push' rather than the 'pull' method with emphasis on transparency; and the intelligence agencies operating on the principle of "responsibility to provide information".

- Possibility of lateral posting of officers (on deputation) within various components of the organizational structure. This would help better understanding of functional aspects of various agencies and would facilitate smooth planning and conduct of force projection operations.

- Sound and effective coordination mechanism to synthesize and synergise multi agency functions since each of these agencies will have a crucial role to play in the conduct of integrated force projection operations.

- Consistent attempt will have to be made at comprehensive and all encompassing capacity building for such a force. The capacity building should ensure that the aspect of interoperability is kept in mind while procuring weapons, equipment and other stores to be used by various agencies employed in force projection operations.

Proposed Organizational Structure

Before recommending or suggesting any proposed organizational structure to undertake force projection operations it may be apt to emphasize that India is not a member of any military alliance or strategic group; and therefore, it needs to maintain an independent deterrent capability for which it will have to be strong in conventional, asymmetric and nuclear capabilities. Only then can it flex its muscle and venture into the realms of force projection. It will have to fight every future war in an integrated manner besides raising the bar for levels of technology in all its manifestations with a view to add teeth to its defence capabilities. Therefore, a macro level restructuring of the decision making apparatus will have to be undertaken to strengthen the force projection options to assert its rightful dominance in the region.

One such proposed organisation has been shown in the figure placed on next page.

The basis for proposing the said organisation and the tasks envisaged for each of the components have been elaborated in succeeding sub paragraphs.

- **Political and Diplomatic Wing**

    - The vast array of emerging global and regional complexities enjoin upon India to define, announce and promulgate its intent of asserting itself, regionally as well as globally. This necessitates formulation of a force projection doctrine based on an unambiguously defined political directive suitably aided by diplomatic guidelines and objectives. The political components of such an organisation needs representation from a number of ministries since each of these ministerial components

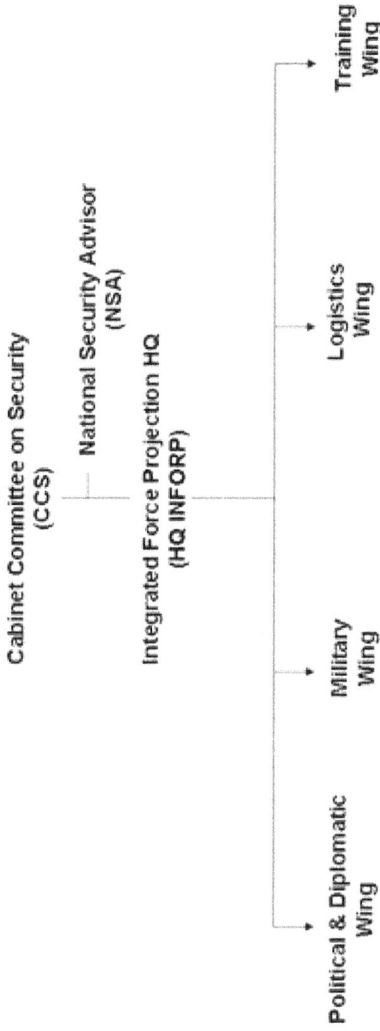

Cabinet Committee on Security (CCS)

National Security Advisor (NSA)

Integrated Force Projection HQ (HQ INFORP)

Political & Diplomatic Wing

Military Wing

Logistics Wing

Training Wing

Note : Organisational Chart of each of these Wings is explained separately) have an important role for successful outcome of force projection operations. Brief description of these components and their task is being dwelled upon hereunder:

- **Ministry of External Affairs (MEA)**

  The Ministry of External Affairs plays a pivotal role in handling the out of area contingencies and disaster management eventualities. It can contribute immensely by way of having an Intelligence Cell, Diplomatic Cell and a Disaster Management Cell. Some of the recommended tasks for these three cells are:-

  - Maintain a data base, including latest maps, in respect of all those countries in the region which may afford an out of area contingency option for India.

  - Ensure continuous and uninterrupted flow of information, especially so, after the initial signs of likelihood of a contingency appear on the horizon.

  - Intelligence Cell of the MEA should have representation from the Research and Analysis Wing (RAW), Intelligence Bureau (IB).

  - The Diplomatic Cell must ensure a close coordination between our embassies, diplomatic missions and Defence Attaches in various countries. The Cell should also serve as a 'information-feed' through detailed analysis of the host country (when OOAC occurs) and its diplomatic negotiations with other global and regional players.

  - MEA should also have a Disaster Management cell that should serve as the nodal agency to coordinate all

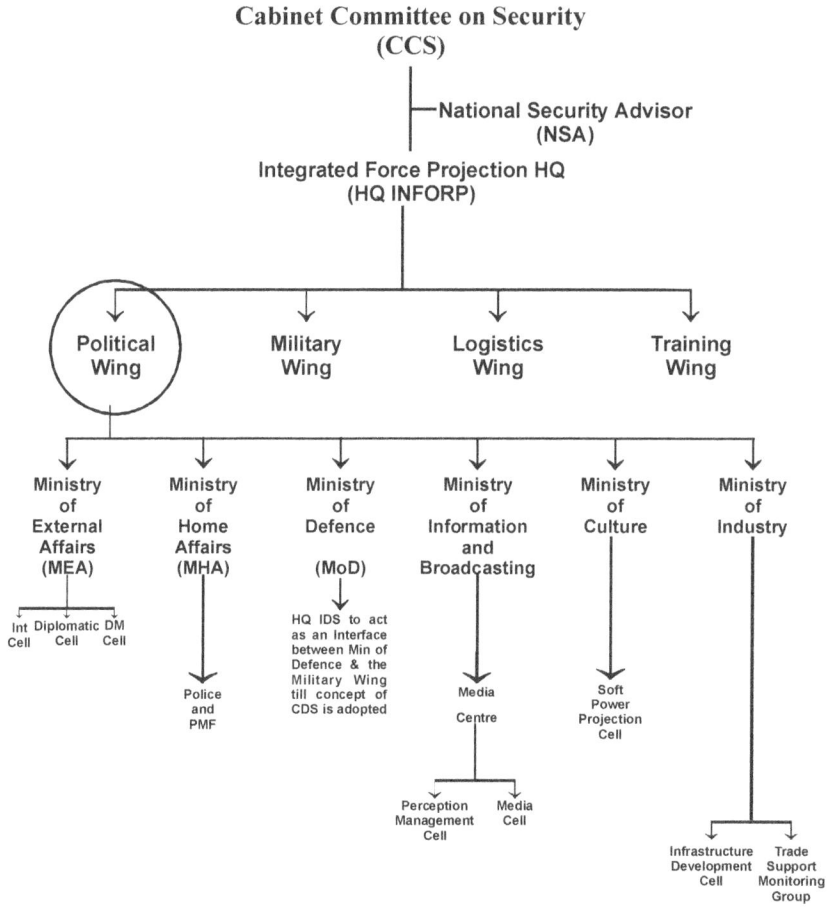

activities related to the induction of the projection force in the target country.

- **Ministry of Home Affairs (MHA)**

Ministry of Home Affairs, though, may not have a direct involvement in terms of contributing any contingents or cells to the out of area contingency force but will have a significant role to play at the time of preparation and launch / induction of such a force. Possible role or tasks that can be performed by MHA are:

  - Provision/requisition of civil hired transport (CHTs) for mobilization of various components of the task force.

  - Allocation of Police and Para Military Force to assist in the launch of the projection force.

  - Possibility of grouping senior Police Officers to accompany the projection force with a view to liaise with the local police of the host country where force projection operations are being launched. This may pay dividends when such operations are being launched in the countries that have a 'colonial' past since there may be some similarity in the police set up in these countries with the set up that exists in India. Such a setup may facilitate the projection force in establishing better support and functional understanding with the host country's law and order machinery.

- **Ministry of Defence**

Ministry of Defence should have a representation in the Political Wing at the Secretarial/Joint Secretarial level to coordinate various activities with other ministerial representatives in the Political Wing. It should also have suitable representation from the Defence Forces by way of nominating retired officers in advisory capacities and serving officers for coordinating the conduct of the entire force projection 'operations' by the military component of the Integrated Force Projection Headquarters. Details of the military component have been discussed separately.

- **Ministry of Information & Broadcasting**

As part of its long-term policy in handling media during the times of crisis, the Information and Broadcasting Ministry (I&B ministry), along with the Home Ministry, plans to start a 24x7 Control Room that will act as a Nerve Centre to receive and disseminate information. The Control Room will be operated by Press Information Bureau during times of crisis. It will be operational throughout the year. The decision was taken at a recent meeting (post Pune Blasts in Feb 2010). The meeting also streamlined various operating procedures. The government has also decided that as soon as a crisis occurs and the National Crisis Management Committee headed by the Cabinet Secretary meets, it should nominate a spokesperson who will interact with the Media on all aspects related to the crisis. The I & B Ministry, through PIB and other organs is expected to facilitate media interaction while the committee will keep the Cabinet Committee on Security (CCS) updated on the developments.[80] When such an attempt is possible to handle the internal security and contingencies/crisis within the territorial confines of the geographical boundary of the nation, similar set up can also be worked out for the purposes of media coverage during out of area contingencies and effect based operations that are launched as part of an integrated force projection operation. The I & B Ministry can have the following

---

[80] Himanshi Dhawan, TNN, "Now a 24 x 7 Media During Crisis", Times of India, New Delhi

organizational set up to cater for the requirements of the force earmarked for projecting the national "interest" in the region:-

- **Media Centre**

   Media centre should be the nodal agency to ensure credible, truthful and authentic dissemination of information. Since force projection operations will always be covered by international media and newsprint, the media centre should have adequately experienced staff with proven maturity and integrity to ensure that "sensationalisation" does not take precedence over "national interests". It should also have a balanced mix of representation in terms of defence correspondents and retired defence officers who have established credentials as defence analysts.

- **Perception Management Cell**

   I & B ministry should also establish a Perception Management Cell that should interact with the local media of the host country where force projection operations are launched. The cell must aim at managing the perceptions of the masses in a subtle manner so that they are convinced of the need for such operations. Successful perception management can act as a catalyst in ensuring favourable outcome of force projection operations. This cell need not wait for the out of area contingency to occur; it should rather be in constant touch with our diplomatic missions and launch its pre-planned programmes without even physically deploying in the target country. The Perception Management Programmes can be aired from home as well as by other friendly nations in the region.

•   **Ministry of Cultural Affairs**

The concept of power projection had, for long, been considered as a military domain. The perception changed only recently when the world realized that effective power projection results only when all elements of a nation's comprehensive national power are applied synergistically with a well defined and spelled out national objective to be achieved. Ministry of Cultural Affairs can contribute handsomely by way of "soft power" projection which is a nascent concept and was added to the "Power Projection" mechanics in early 1990s when Joseph Nye of Harvard University propounded that concept of "Soft Power". Since then, the term is being widely used in international relations. Soft Power, in essence, is the ability to obtain what you want, by using the concepts of "cooption and attraction". Primary currencies of the soft power are values, culture, policies, traditions, public diplomacy, reputation etc. If these be the primary currencies then Ministry of Cultural Affairs ought to be the "custodian" of these currencies and therefore, should step in to fruitfully and favourably give attention, encouragement and active support to those aspects and products of our society which the world would find attractive. To project India's soft power, concurrently with hard power, the Cultural Affairs Ministry should exploit the resources of the state as well as non-state actors, both, within as also, outside the country.

It is crucial to understand that Hard and Soft Powers will always complement each other's efforts because they both aim at projecting the nation's comprehensive power, even though the means employed by them are totally different. Soft Power resources tend to be associated with the 'cooptive end' of the spectrum of behaviour whereas hard power resources are associated with the 'coercive aspects' or command behaviour. A judiciously ground paste of hard and soft power will certainly be an effective recipe for success in force projection ventures.

- **Military Wing**

It has been abundantly discussed in some of the previous chapters that in the present geo-strategic environment India needs to look outwards to stake its rightful claim as a regional power. It must focus beyond it's land and maritime frontiers to announce its emergence on the global and regional power dynamics for which it needs to have a credibly strong military that should work on the principle of 'integrated response' to all crisis and contingencies. The Army should have Rapid Deployment capabilities in terms of Force Projection Division as shown in the figure and must have state of the art weapons and equipment; the Navy should acquire capabilities that would allow it to present a minimum threshold of resistance and deterrence in the Indian Ocean Region (IOR) from the Coast of Africa in the West to the Malacca Straits and beyond in the East; and the Air Force must acquire capabilities to dominate the air space and enhance its strategic reach. There is also a need for enhancing the sea and airlift capabilities for rapidly launching out of area contingency operations. The military objectives that each of the three services should strive to achieve with regard to force projection operations should be as follows:-

- **Army**

    o   Maintain adequate capability to ensure security and territorial integrity of all our island territories.

    o   Keep our extended neighbourhood under surveillance to discern any activities inimical to our security interests.

Cabinet Committee on Security
(CCS)

National Security Advisor
(NSA)

Integrated Force Projection HQ
(HQ INFORP)

- Political Wing
- Military Wing
- Logistics Wing
- Training Wing

Army — Navy — Air Force

Force Projection Division

Navy:
- Carrier Battle Group (CBG)
- Amph Lift Force (LSTs)
- Maritime Recce Group (MRG)

Air Force:
- Strategic Air Lift Wing
- Space Cell
- Heptrs
- Air to Air Refuellers

Satellite Recce Group

Force Projection Division:
- Air Assault Brigade
- Light Armd Brigade
- Combat Support Elements

Air Assault Brigade:
- 03 Mech Bns 02 Inf Bns & 1 SFF
- 01 Mech Coy

Light Armd Brigade:
- Armd Regt (1)
- Mech Bns (2)

Marine Brigade
- 02 Inf Bns
- 01 SFF Bn

Aviation Squadron
- 01 Attack Heptr Fit
- 01 Recce Heptr Fit

Strategic Air Lift Wing:
- Heavy Tac ACs (HETAC)
- Medium Tac ACs (METAC)
- Light Tac ACs (LETAC)

Heptrs:
- Utility Flight
- Recce Flight
- UAV Flight

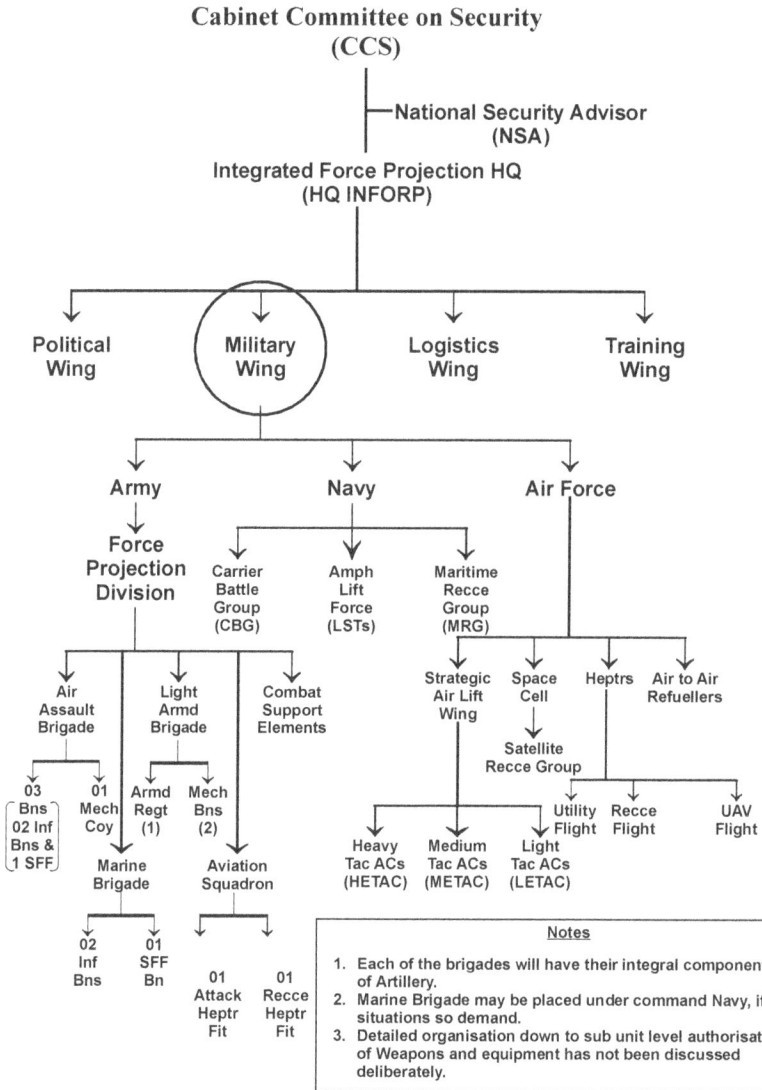

Notes
1. Each of the brigades will have their integral component of Artillery.
2. Marine Brigade may be placed under command Navy, if situations so demand.
3. Detailed organisation down to sub unit level authorisation of Weapons and equipment has not been discussed deliberately.

- o Be prepared for military intervention and/or assistance on request from neighbouring countries or other countries that request for each assistance.

- o Provide immediate assistance for Disaster Management .

- o Build capability to operate for prolonged duration in the host country, should the situation so demand.

- o Promote regular and frequent military to military cooperation with countries of interest.

- o Be prepared to participate in UN missions.

- o Build capabilities to launch surgical offensive operations in the immediate neighbourhood, should our national security be threatened, either overtly or covertly, by any nation.

- **Navy**

  - o Exercise sea control in the Arabian Sea, Bay of Bengal and at the selected entry and exit points to the IOR. This would extend from the Malacca straits in the East to Straits of Hormuz and Bab-al-Mandab in the west.

  - o Protect India's EEZ against illegal exploitation.

  - o Meet contingencies in the neighbourhood such as military assistance to Mauritius, Seychelles, Sri Lanka, Maldives etc.

  - o Gain confidence of IOR littorals.

  - o Assist in disaster management and relief operations.

  - o Safeguard India's mercantile marine and sea-borne trade through the SLOCs.

o   Use Navy as an effective instrument of India's foreign policy by generating goodwill through maritime diplomacy.

o   Develop healthy maritime partnerships to showcase India's force projection capabilities to the world.

o   Build capabilities to operate with multinational forces, thereby cementing India's emerging profile as a nation that has potential to project its military might as and when situation demands so.

o   Continue contribution to UN peace keeping operations.

· **Air Force**

o   Maintain adequate air capability to safeguard our off-shore assets, EEZ and SLOCs.

o   Achieve capability to secure our island territories.

o   Maintain strategic airlift capability to mobilize our forces for the intended out of area contingency operations.

o   Be prepared to assist in disaster management and relief operations in the region.

o   Have capability to evacuate Indian Diaspora from any part of the world should their safety be compromised at any stage.

o   Have suitable contingency plans for assistance in our immediate neighbourhood, should any formal request be received from these nations.

o   Participate in UN Peace Keeping Operations in any part of the globe.

- **Organisational Recourse**

  It has now been accepted not only in the corridors of Power in India but throughout the world that Revolution in Military Affairs (RMA) can only be achieved through an integrated approach. The demands of interoperability can only be met through integration and jointmanship and not by triphibious warfare doctrines or independently evolved procedures of the three services. Only collaborative efforts and synergized solutions hold key to RMA and an integrated response mechanism. The issue of having a Chief of Defence Staff (CDS) therefore re-emerges for deliberation and consideration since CDS system will fulfil the need to have an integrated command structure at the apex level. However, this aspect of CDS is not being dwelled any further since it needs an in depth debate and deliberation at the highest levels of decision making.

  Till the concept of CDS fully evolves, the Force Projection Division should function under the Headquarters Integrated Defence Staff with the command function under the CISC. The recommended organizational structure of the military wing of the force projection set up in India has been shown in the figures(*page 146*). Brief explanation of the structure has been given in the succeeding sub paragraphs.

- **Army**

  The Army component should have a Force Projection Division with one Air Assault Brigade, One Amphibious Brigade, One Light Armoured Brigade and an Aviation Squadron. Besides that, the necessary combat support services and elements will have to be grouped to enable the division to be self contained, at least for 90 days, by which time the supply chain management system would be fully effective.

The Air Assault Brigade is a significant force multiplier and can serve as the Rapid Deployment component of the Force Projection Division. This Brigade will have the support of the integral heli lift capability of the Force Projection Division to ensure its rapid deployment in the peripheral contingencies around the Indian sub continent. The Brigade should have atleast two specially air trained infantry battalions and one Special Force Battalion. The integral Artillery Regiment of the Brigade will provide intimate fire support. The Brigade should also have a dedicated Mechanized Infantry Company to provide the necessary fire power and mobility needed for shock action that is so very crucial for gaining initial foothold in the target country. Necessary combat support elements that are grouped with a fighting formation will remain integral to Air Assault Brigade also. The tasks assigned to this brigade could be to secure a foothold, establish an airhead, secure threatened island territories, rescue power centres, capture Vital Areas/Vital Points (VAs/VPs) and/ or assist in disaster management activities.

The Marine Brigade of the Force Projection Division should have amphibious capabilities with the necessary transportation assets being held with the Indian Navy. The Brigade should have two infantry battalions and one Special Forces Battalion who should all be trained in amphibious warfare. The Brigade should also have a Marine Commandos (MARCOS) complement to undertake special operations prior to, or during the launch of the amphibious force. This brigade should have the capability to remain self contained for 30-45 days. Fire support should be provided by the integral artillery regiment while the aviation assets available to the Force Projection Division will be on call to provide the necessary air support; both for operations as well as for logistics back up.

Light Armoured Brigade with an armoured regiment and two mechanized infantry battalions will form the third major component of the division. This brigade will be particularly useful in plains and in littoral regions. The Force Projection Division must have its integral Aviation Squadron with an Attack Helicopter flight and a Reconnaissance flight. This squadron will provide the necessary support to all the three formations (Brigades).

The combat support services and elements, as applicable to the division, would also form an integral part of the Force Projection Division. Besides that, the division should have the inherent capabilities to absorb additional forces should there be a requirement for more troops to address the out of area contingency.

• **Navy**

In order to perform the maritime force projection role the Navy must possess the capability to project credible power at a considerable distance from one's shores. This would necessitate building up of Carrier Battle Group (CBG) capability of atleast three carriers so that one CBG each is available to operate off the East and West Coasts while one is undergoing routine maintenance. The Marine Brigade of the Force Projection Division should have the flexibility of being employed either by the Army or by the Navy in consonance with the need of the hour. This maritime brigade will have troops trained in amphibious warfare.

The Amphibious Lift Force should have a balance mix of LST (L) and LST (M) to ensure speedy lift for the mobilization and deployment of the mechanized component of the task force. Long term acquisition of an Advanced Amphibious Assault Vehicle (AAAV) and air-cushioned landing crafts should also be studied. There may be a requirement to group submarines and fast attack aircrafts with stealth capability.

The surveillance group should have surface component as well as air component to ensure surveillance and reconnaissance. The Maritime Reconnaissance aircrafts should be capable of carrying anti-ship missiles to ensure timely engagement of hostile vessels that may engage the projection force during its move to the intended area of operations. The need for an autonomous logistic support for such a task force cannot be overemphasized. Concomitantly, the possibility of utilizing the merchant fleet, fishing crafts and associated port infrastructure will also need to be considered holistically. By focusing on building force projection capabilities Navy would be able to exercise effective sea control and sea denial operations in furtherance of India's regional aspirations. In addition, it will automatically strengthen and hone up its disaster management capabilities and credibility in undertaking UN peace keeping operations as part of multi-lateral force.

• **Air Force**

Air power in today's warfare has reached the status of the dominant factor that has a determining effect on the outcome of any conflict. It is true that air power may not win a war by itself alone; but without it no major war can be won.[81] The logic applies to the force projection operations also. Air Force will have to play a significant

---

[81] Air Cmde Jasjit Singh, 'Air Power in Modern Warfare', (New Delhi: Lance International, 1985; p-xxi.

role in the force projection domain since air power, willy-nilly, has become the currency of strategic strength of a nation. It has the attributes to respond rapidly with fire power and mobility to address any out of area contingency, besides addressing the conventional concerns. It has immense power projection capabilities in terms of long range strike capability, strategic aircraft, precision munitions, real time intelligence et el. Therefore, IAF will have to 'forge for itself an entity which would be armed and trained to meet most contingencies'.[82]

In terms of strategic airlift we need to enhance our capabilities to cater for force projection and disaster relief operations. Ideally the force must comprise a balance mix of Heavy, Medium and Light Transport aircrafts with payload capacities of 40-45 tons, 15-20 tons and 04 to 06 tons respectively. While the exact numbers of squadrons in each of these variants may be deliberately debated at appropriate fora, recommended proportion for launching one divisional size projection force could be three to four Heavy Transport Aircraft (HETAC) and Medium Transport Aircraft (METAC) squadrons each and about four to five Light Transport Aircraft (LTA) squadrons. Such an airlift capability should be able to cater for conventional needs as well as the out of area contingencies including disasters, natural calamities and evaluation of Indian Diaspora.

Another crucial requirement for addressing force projection commitments would be in terms of air to air refuellers. The IAF has already acquired six aerial refuellers and there are plans to acquire few more

---

[82] Air Cmde SP Tyagi, An IAF for the future: Some Considerations', Strategic Analysis, Dec 1997, P1343.

refuellers to enhance our global reach. Induction of these aircrafts in the inventory serves dual purpose in terms of their utility as cargo planes. This dual role capability enhances our strategic lift capability and gives us a global reach and a multiple choice of options. These aircrafts have already been put to test in joint exercises to stage our fighter aircrafts to Alaska, South Africa and France.

Helicopters constitute the other inescapable requirement for any force projection mission. Due to the versatility and ease of operation of a helicopter, and given the diverse terrain in which it can perform multitude of tasks, the helicopters play a major role in supporting the out of area contingencies. Hence a substantial allocation in our helicopter assets needs to be envisaged. The IAF has already initiated the process for procurement of Medium Lift Helicopters (MLH). Acquisition of these MLHs is in keeping with the overall plan for enhancement of 'strategic reach' of the IAF.[83] Concurrent with these acquisitions goes the undisputed need to be self sufficient; and therefore the requirement of promoting indigenous development. The self sufficiency in terms of required number of helicopters will facilitate dedicated allocation of attack helicopters as well as utility helicopters for the purposes of supporting the force projection contingents.

Space, as an added dimension, is increasingly being recognized as the new high ground that needs to be exploited in the 21st century. In the past, ships and aircrafts were used to shrink oceans and compress geographical distances, but today it is the space that is offering the additional geo-strategic dimensions to the

---

[83] Air Chief Mshl SP Tyagi, "Role of the IAF in the Changing Regional Security Environment; NISDA Security conference 2005 Inaugural Address.

space-faring nations. Space is being fully recognized as a medium which must be gainfully exploited for strategic dividends. The synthesis of air power weapon systems with space based, satellite mounted support systems have provided us with precision guidance, accurate navigation, real-time intelligence and effective communication capabilities. Air power has now emerged as an "Aerospace Power" taking warfare in the fourth dimensions and to the last frontier of human concerns.[84] The Force Projection set up in India should also have a dedicated organization that should cater for satellite reconnaissance and provide near real time large scale surveillance and assessment with the help of Real Time Multispectral Satellite Sensors (RTMSS). The space cell should also ensure battlefield transparency to the commanders with the help of ESM, ECM & ECCM measures. Space assets thus, can be powerful terrestrial force multipliers. The force enhancement mission that can add teeth to the projection force using space as a medium are navigation, communications, missile warning, weather and intelligence support. Synthesis and integration of these dimensions with other components will have to be coordinated at appropriate levels.

- **Logistics Array**

Just like any other operation, the success of force projection also hinges on a sound and effective logistics support. The infrastructural development and administrative set up will have to cater for multi-dimensional options for launching the force as well as supporting its prolonged commitment in the target

---

[84] Air Cmde NB Singh, Air Power in the New Millennium, New Delhi, Manas Publications, 200; p 11.

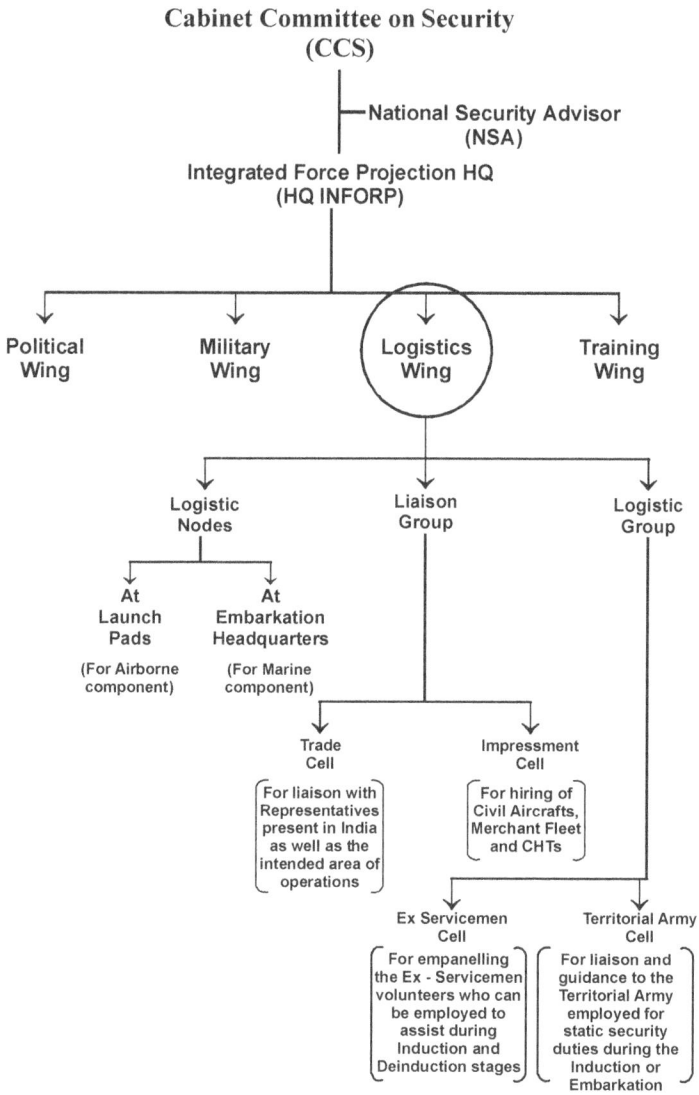

area. Thus following issues will have to be looked into at the launch pads (air field), Embarkation HQ and at the mounting bases:-

o Adequate storage for pre-positioning arms, ammunition and equipment earmarked for out of area contingencies.

o Technical accommodation and hangers.

o Cargo loading vehicles for ships and air crafts.

o Recovery aids and safety services.

o Ware houses for supplies.

o Accommodation for manpower.

o Traffic Management Organisation.

o Hospital facilities.

o Storage for war waging reserves.

The option of utilizing the ex-servicemen and Territorial Army personnel for manning the logistic cells also needs to be deliberated upon. Once a successful model is evolved and trial-evaluated, it will reduce pressure on the combatants who will always be a "Secure resource", more so because of immense commitment of our Forces (especially army) in the Low Insecurity Conflict Operations and asymmetric warfare.

• **Training**

No organization, be it in defence or in a civil set up, can boast of proficiency in its assigned role and mission without putting its employees through a well chalked out training programme. Force Projection Operations also suffer from same dilemma i.e. how to organize sound and effective training for various

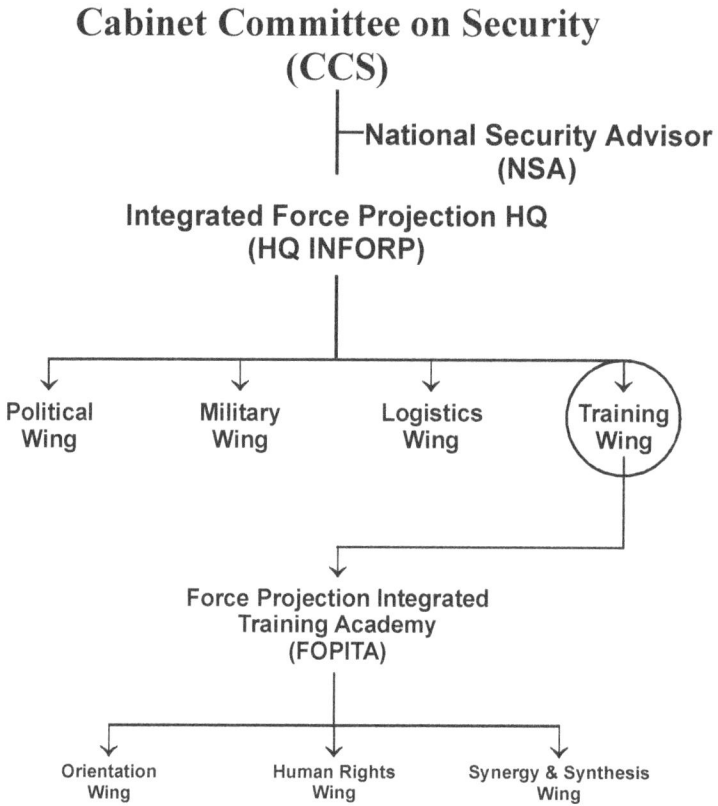

components. It is therefore recommended that a Force Projection Integrated Training Academy (FOPITA) be commissioned to cater for integrated training. The academy can have independent programmes for Officers and Personnel Below Officers Rank (PBOR). The academy can have following wings:

o   **Orientation Wing**

Officers and men from all components of Projection Force should be subjected to a four weeks Orientation Programme to Study international relations, international maritime laws, UN resolutions, Country Studies, humanitarian laws and other similar subjects.

o   **Human Rights (HR) Wing**

The force needs to be exposed to importance of Human Rights and various provisions associated with them lest they commit gross HR violations that may lead to international ramifications and criticism regarding the conduct of the Projection Force.

o   **Synergy and Synthesis Wing**

As the name suggests, this wing will have to focus on synergy and jointmanship issues. Need for a cohesive and synthesized bonding among all the constituents will have to be emphasized during training itself. Brief awareness about each other's strength and weeknesses will facilitate in generating a healthy and viscous working atmosphere among various components in the projection force.

· **Communication Setup**

· **Services Required:** Tri Service Operations need a wide spectrum of communication services in order to be effective. The ideal situation would be a mix of triple play services in terms of Voice, Data and Video. It is through voice that immediate and effective Command and Control can be exercised but exhaustive passage of detailed instructions and voluminous reports is facilitated through data. The options of using video conferencing facilities provide a convenient alternative to various components of the Projection Force to coordinate and fine tune various drills and procedures. This would obviate the requirement of frequent move of commanders and staff to attend various meetings and conferences for coordination.

- **Interoperability:** Time, energy and resources are thus saved by use of these 'triple play services'. However, unlike a single service scenario where all features are fully integrated in an integrated operation environment, the 'triple play services of Voice, Video & Data' are provided by respective services and therefore need to be interoperable with each other. The same will thus need a standard data dictionary and a common data format/ structure/ architecture to be put in place.

- **Bandwidth:** The existing scales of Bandwidth (BW) within the three services may be adequate to meet the individual service specific requirements of each service, for voice & data. However, in an integrated scenario there would be an extensive requirement of transmitting imagery including maps which would entail a very high capacity of BW which will need to be factored into.

- **Data Paradigm:** Security of the Data being transmitted assumes significance, and ideally, all seven layers of the OIS model should be providing security. However, the trend at present is that security solutions are provided only for the transport layer and sometimes at the application level.

- **Different Media:** The communication support provided should be with the mix of different types of communication media, each providing redundancy to the other. In a typically integrated scenario like force projection, satellite, though may be an ideal means of communication, yet it is best suited as a back up measure in view of the constraints of bandwidth. Wherever feasible high bandwidth capacity, using optic fibre cable, should be built in and back up provided through satellite media. This option would be ideal during the pre induction stage when various forces have to mobilise from different locations and have to concentrate at the launch bases and embarkation ports. Wherever satellite is envisaged to be used as a primary means of communication, high capacity transponders must be factored in.

- **Communication on the Move and Static Communication:** The requirements of communication support that should be provided on the move and those required at static locations are entirely different and at times do not complement each other. However, an effort must be made to select such a medium of communication which meets the requirements of mobile communication which is light weight, portable, ruggedized and lends itself to easy deployability, while at the same time meeting the requirements of high capacity and stability of communication which is required for static locations.

- **Flatter Organisations vs Hierarchical Structure:** The communication requirements for force projection entails simultaneous passage of information and messages which lend it to flatter organisation and the communication support must be geared up accordingly. This will lead to some organisational re-structuring to be carried out to replace the hierarchical structure and will give way to an era of networking.

- **Government and Non Government Agency:** With the proliferation of communication and IT Services, the expertise in various sectors lies with the Govt agencies and at times with certain non Govt agencies. As such players from these non Govt agencies also should be actively involved in meeting the communication requirements of the communication support for force projection operations.

- **Use of Public Networks:** Internet and Intranet of respective services are extremely powerful mediums of communications which are not being optimally exploited. The same have a large reach and by taking care of certain security constraints, the services can use such networks for passing voice, data and video communication support during out of area contingency operations in view of their extended reach and ready availability.

- **Security & Cryptographic Cover:** There is a need to provide security solution for communication services engineered for integrated operations scenario. However, provisioning of the security solution should be fast, should be in a time bound manner and should be in speed with the solutions being provided in the cyber domain.

- **Common Standards and Protocols:** At present the plethora of communication and IT equipment being inducted in the three services does not have common standards or protocols. The same are imperative if the networks are to talk to each other and inventory has to be reduced to ensure an effective supply chain management in respect of communication equipment and peripherals.

CONCLUSION

We are what we repeatedly do. Excellence, then, is not an act but a habit.

- Aristotle

India, of late, has reassessed its position globally as well as regionally. It has rightly put economic renaissance at the centre of its foreign policy formulation suitably aided by diplomatic expeditions at strengthening bilateral and multilateral relations within the region as well as at the global plane. It looks in detail at the geo-strategic and geo-political spectrum to play a significant role in international relations and has started introspecting and weighing all dimensions of complex geo strategic equilibrium and international relationships. Government's attempts to prioritise highly complex and sometimes competing global and regional objectives have apparently commenced and have started bearing fruit. The West, as also the regional web of South Asian countries, have been exhibiting interest in India's growing stature as a dominant regional power. Mutual suspicions amongst the neighbours have started waning with dawning of the realisation for an over-arching and quintessential requirement for stability and security, even at the sub-regional level. Countries in this region are striving to go beyond confidence-building measures and preventive diplomacy and are willing to adopt a proactive stance to announce that they would not hesitate to step out and project force to help their regional neighbours in the event of a crisis.

There may be opinions that democratic states should avoid exercising the force projection options. But without disputing their viewpoint, it may be apt and apposite to sneak a look into the very concept of nation states and the use of various instruments of statecraft by these nation states to safeguard their strategic interests. It would plainly emerge, and rather loud and clear, that all instruments of national power can be used by the nations to achieve objectives that are vital for national security. In fact, nations have the liberty to blend their strategic interests and democratic norms, or any other form of governance, to protect their vital national interests. So India is well within its rights to unilaterally take recourse to force projection option for furthering its national interests. In fact, India's foreign policy has the long-term vision of living in peace with its neighbours and does not seek relations to be held hostage on any singular issues with any of its neighbours. This perhaps, explains why India's world vision is expansive and seeks to promote peaceful cooperation and coexistence rather than confrontation. But within this paradigm, it is equally significant for us to proclaim that India will assert and aver itself comprehensively to serve its vital national interests in the region. It would not hesitate to adopt the politics of persuasion and diplomatic rendezvous in dealing with the neighbourhood crises that may dent its credibility as an emerging regional power.

The study has made an endeavour to bring forth various nuances of force projection and how they affect India. It was aimed at evoking and inducing certain thoughts on force projection by India with a view to provoke and inflame the strategists, think tanks and intelligentsia to evolve a credible Force Projection Doctrine for the country. It may therefore be appropriate to discuss, deliberate and debate the force projection options for India at various fora to facilitate speedy and timely formulation of the doctrine.

www.ingramcontent.com/pod-product-compliance
Lightning Source LLC
Chambersburg PA
CBHW060421100426
42812CB00030B/3264/J